SUICIDE

How

God

Sustained

a Family

SUICIDE
How

God

Sustained

a Family

DALE A. BYERS

REGULAR BAPTIST PRESS
1300 North Meacham Road
Schaumburg, Illinois 60173-4888

CATALOGING IN PUBLICATION DATA
Byers, Dale A., 1937–
    Suicide : how God sustained a family / Dale A. Byers.
        p.   cm.
ISBN 0-87227-146-3
    1. Consolation.   2. Bereavement—Religious aspects—Christianity.
3. Suicide—Religious aspects—Christianity.   4. Byers, Kerry, d.
1988. I. Title.
BV4905.2.B94   1991
248.8'6—dc20   91-8836
                                                                                        CIP

© 1991
Regular Baptist Press
Schaumburg, Illinois

DEDICATION

It is with joy this book is dedicated to
Kevin, Scott, Paul and **John,**
our four living sons.
They are honorable men
who have brought many fond
and wonderful memories to their parents.

ACKNOWLEDGMENTS

We acknowledge with appreciation the quotations taken from

Encyclopedia of 7,000 Illustrations: Signs of the Times by Paul Lee Tan. Copyright 1979 by Assurance Publishers.

"No More!" "Thank God! No More!": The Seven No Mores of Revelation by David Otis Fuller. Copyright by The Institute For Biblical Textual Studies.

The Best of A.W. Tozer edited by Warren W. Wiersbe. Copyright 1979 by Baker Book House.

How to Build an Evangelistic Church by John R. Bisagno. Copyright 1972 by Broadman Press.

Close to His Majesty by David C. Needham. Copyright 1987 by Multnomah Press, Portland, Oregon 97266. Used by permission.

The Disciplines of Life by V. Raymond Edman. Copyright 1948 by Victor Books/SP Publications, Inc.

Root of the Righteous by A. W. Tozer. Copyright by Christian Publications. Used by permission.

We would also like to acknowledge Hattie Walker for granting permission to use her poem "The Savior Walks Beside Me."

We also acknowledge the quotation taken from *God's Provision for Holy Living* by W. Culbertson. Moody Bible Institute of Chicago. Moody Press. Used by permission.

CONTENTS

And I will give thee the treasures of darkness, and hidden riches of secret places, that thou mayest know that I, the LORD, which call thee by thy name, am the God of Israel (Isaiah 45:3).

INTRODUCTION

My heart was rejoicing as the church service closed in that little Jamaican church. It was the first time for me to minister in a foreign culture and, oh, what a blessing! As we stepped outside that primitive little church snuggled under the tropical trees and dense undergrowth alongside the road that winds around those Jamaican mountains, we were aware that this humble spot was precious to God and that we were on holy ground. The pastor turned out the lights of the church and walked toward the parsonage, which sat behind this little sanctuary. I remained stationary, waiting for something that would give me bearings as to my location. Suddenly I was aware of the heavy darkness that surrounded that Jamaican place of worship. There was a noticeable absence of street lights and passing automobiles. There were no flashing marquees or billboards nor even the beams of light that stream from the comforts of home. It seemed totally dark.

Suddenly I lifted my eyes heavenward and was awestruck by the beauties above me. Never had I seen stars so big and so bright; they were like huge gems lying in a case of black velvet. It was almost disappointing when the parsonage lights came on and again we had our earthly bearings. Indeed, there are treasures of darkness.

That same week I walked along the shoreline of the Caribbean Sea with James Chambers, a Jamaican friend. Another pastor had asked if I might talk with James and encourage him spiritually. While we left the prints of our bare feet in the white sand along the blue-green waters of the sea, he poured out his heart to me concerning the utter discouragement that followed the death of his eleven-year-old daughter. He had been so devastated he felt he could continue no longer. Then his fourteen-year-old son lay down beside him in bed with these words of encouragement and exhortation: "You have to let her go, Daddy. She is in Heaven with Jesus. We have got to let her go!"

James did begin a period of recovery, but it was short-lived. The son who had exhorted him was tragically killed in an accident at school. James had lost two children in a very short period of time!

Later James came to the United States because he was losing much of his eyesight. The American doctors at the clinic told him he should learn to live with what eyesight he had.

If anyone had ever needed the grace of God in his life, James did. He is a believer in Christ, and his love and faith are being measured as few men experience.

I made a feeble attempt to comfort him that day and encouraged him to trust God and to look to the Lord Jesus every day for strength. We have become close friends; and I have called him, written to him and prayed regularly for God's overcoming power in his life.

Less than a year after my return from Jamaica I, too, was to learn what darkness is all about. God had blessed our home with five sons. The desire of my heart has always been for my children to love the Lord Jesus. It was my joy as a pastor to see all of them profess Christ and follow the Lord in baptism. But our third son became wayward and rejected the principles upon which I attempted to build my home. Kerry's life was a downward spiral that we could not reverse.

Even though he lived in the same city, he did not live at home. Following a two-year stint in the military, he was divorced and disappointed with life. He then committed suicide on what would have been his third wedding anniversary. We did not immediately realize he was missing; however, after a ten-day lapse of time my two youngest sons found his body in a little woods near the parsonage.

The darkness of that hour and the days that followed have enveloped our family much like the darkness enveloped that little Jamaican church. We have always been a close family, and this darkness—such as we had never known before—drew us even closer together.

My words to James had come so easily: "Trust God, James, and look to Him for daily strength." Now I had to learn how hard it sometimes is to look up when we have lost our earthly bearings in the darkness.

May I say at the onset, I do trust God; and whatever has happened, God knew all about it before it came to pass. God has been faithful! His promises remain true, and His people have been wonderfully kind to me and my family. I have no bitterness, resentment or doubt of God. I have only a deep hurt and a new awareness of how dense the darkness can become.

As a young man I was an offset printing pressman. At times while I worked the night shift during the summer months, I never saw the night sky. Those were times when the heavens were always light to me; darkness was something I did not observe. The 6:00 P.M. to 5:00 A.M. shifts sheltered me from the night scenes. But only during the night scenes are we permitted to observe the heavenly beauties above us.

Our great God also has heavenly beauties that we observe only during the dark night seasons of our lives. Only then are we permitted to fathom the fullness and the glories of our great God and Savior.

"I will give thee the treasures of darkness." This message is not about darkness and death. It is about light and life. It is intended to help those going through the shadow of death to gaze into the heavenly beauties of our glorious Redeemer.

The Soul's Anchors

The night is dark, but God, my God,
    Is here and in command,
And sure am I, when morning breaks,
    I shall be at the land.
And since I know the darkness is
    To Him as sunniest day,
I'll cast the anchor Patience out,
    And wish—but wait for day.

Fierce drives the storm, but wind and waves
    Within His hand are held,
And trusting His omnipotence,
    My fears are sweetly quelled.
If wrecked, I'm in His faithful grasp,
    I'll trust Him though He slay;
So, letting go the anchor Faith,
    I'll wish—but wait for day.

Still seem the moments dreary, long?
    I rest upon the Lord;
I muse on His "eternal years"
    And feast upon His word;
His promises so rich and great,
    Are my support and stay;
I'll drop the anchor Hope ahead,
    And wish—but wait for day.

O Wisdom infinite, O Light
    And Love supreme, divine,
How can I feel one fluttering doubt
    In hands so dear as Thine!
I'll lean on Thee, my best beloved,
    My heart on Thy heart lay;
And casting out the anchor Love,
    I'll wish—and wait for day.
                  —*Helen E. Brown*
                  As published in the
                  Grace Broadcaster
                  (May–June 1968)

CHAPTER 1

In the Darkness of Death Shines the Radiance of the Resurrection

After Kerry's death my wife, three of my sons and I began the very difficult task of sorting through Kerry's personal items. We discovered that we had saved many trinkets and mementos of all five boys. Some of the little keepsakes and belongings had to go. For many people, material things are what life is all about; but the Bible reminds us that "a man's life consisteth not in the abundance of the things which he possesseth" (Luke 12:15).

As I picked up some of his belongings, my first thoughts were, "We can't throw that away. He will need it later on." My wife similarly would think for a second, "His children will enjoy seeing this someday." However, time and again we were brought back to reality; Kerry would not need these things, and he would have no children to see these "treasures." Our son's earthly life was completed in only twenty-five short years.

Death is a sobering reality. As finite humans we attempt to reason it away. We pigeonhole it to the lives of others. We do not want to accept death for ourselves or our loved ones. The answer to our reluctance is to see death from God's perspective, not from any earthly point of view. When the darkness of death is overwhelming, we must lift our eyes heavenward and see the bright hope of the resurrection. Listen to what Christ has promised:

> *I am the resurrection, and the life: he that believeth in me, though he were dead, yet shall he live: and whosoever liveth and believeth in me shall never die. Believest thou this? (John 11:25, 26).*

The world tells us that death is the last note, that there is no more song at the grave. But the place where the world loses all hope and joy is where Christ gives victory.

> *O death, where is thy sting? O grave, where is thy victory? The sting of death is sin; and the strength of sin is the law. But thanks be to God, which giveth us the victory through our Lord Jesus Christ (1 Corinthians 15:55–57).*

Perhaps it seems strange that this book begins at the resurrection. Why do I not wait until the end, since death is the "last enemy" to be destroyed (1 Corinthians 15:26)? The answer is that the resurrection is the place where we *must* begin. It is the starting place for our comfort, our consolation and the power to climb life's mountains (Ephesians 1:19, 20). The resurrection is the starting point for our healing, our help and our hope. Death is only a rest in the music. More song is going on right now. Much more song is to follow.

The resurrection of the dead is one of the foundation stones of the Christian faith. It is not until the physical death of a loved one or the threat of death to our own life that we realize how glorious and bright the resurrection is. That truth is not learned in the sunny skies and comforts of life. The apostle Paul's goal was to learn that truth practically. The desire of his heart was this:

> *That I may know him, and the power of his*

*resurrection, and the fellowship of his suffer-
ings, being made conformable unto his death
(Philippians 3:10).*

The resurrection of Jesus Christ sets Christianity apart
from every other religion. Buddha, Confucius, Stalin and every
other prominent figure on earth has followed the course of the
earth and died; only Jesus Christ conquered death. And perhaps no other event in history is as thoroughly documented as
the resurrection of the Lord Jesus Christ.[1]

But I am not writing a mere apologetic for the Christian
faith. I am writing to hurting hearts. Since it is true that Christ
arose from the grave, we derive our comfort through the great
resurrection promises He has given us.

*And God hath both raised up the Lord, and
will also raise up us by his own power (1 Corinthians 6:14).*

The Lord Himself said, "Because I live, ye shall live
also" (John 14:19). As surely as Christ arose from the grave,
those who believe on Him shall also live forever.

The Bible identifies the Lord Jesus as the bright and
morning star (Revelation 22:16). What a description! After the
long dark night, that bright light appears in the heavens. Peter
also wrote about his own impending death (2 Peter 1:14, 15)
and then recalled the day on the Mount of Transfiguration
when he saw Jesus in His transcendent glory:

*We have also a more sure word of prophecy;
whereunto ye do well that ye take heed, as
unto a light that shineth in a dark place,
until the day dawn, and the day star arise in
your hearts (2 Peter 1:19).*

Think of it—"A light that shineth in a dark place." You
may now be in a place of awesome darkness that is heavy and

frightening; but the resurrection of the Lord Jesus Christ is a bright and glorious light.

The Bible assures us that when Christ appears, a great reunion of those who have died in Christ will take place with those who are still living at the time (1 Thessalonians 4:13–18). We are told that while we as believers may sorrow in this life over the separation from saved loved ones, we sorrow not as others who have no hope. There will be a reunion, and what comfort this should give us.

My mind recalls so distinctly the day I picked up our children at the Christian school when we lived in Indianapolis. As usual Kerry was the first of my sons to come rushing out the school doors. He bounced into the backseat with his usual burst of energy. When he leaned over the back of my seat, I noticed tears in his eyes. It was evident he had been crying. Almost immediately he said, "Dad, I know I have said this before, but today I really got saved." The Life Action Ministries had conducted the chapel services, and God used that group to bring Kerry to know Christ as his Savior. How that day has since been a comfort to our hearts and has encouraged us with hope for that day when we shall meet again.

How vivid is the memory of my son going off to kindergarten. He would walk about fifty yards to the end of the driveway and wait for the school bus. As it would pull to a stop and open its huge doors, Kerry would put down his lunch pail, turn around and look toward the house and then raise both arms over his head and wave like an athlete doing jumping jacks. Then I would step outside and wave back in identical motion. This became our special signal, and it marked our greetings and partings.

Also vivid in my memory is the day Kerry left for the army. I can still see the bus pulling up to the depot and its wide doors opening to take him away. How my heart ached. Just before he entered the bus, I stepped out where he could see me and gave him our old signal.

When he returned home from Germany, our family went to O'Hare International Airport in Chicago to pick him up.

We arrived early and watched as the jets brought people together from all over the world. What a reunion they were having. People from such places as Japan, Norway, Africa, China and Germany were all being delivered to this one spot. How our emotions were kindled as we watched loved ones greet and embrace. Then came the arrival of our son. How eagerly we waited to see him. As he walked up the narrow passageway leading from the plane, I stepped out where he could see me, placed both hands over my head and gave him our old signal. What people must have thought about that weird man waving his hands over his head in such a manner!

The day we left the body of our son at the cemetery I wanted to stop the car, get out and give him our parting salute; but I knew he was not there. A day will come, however, when Jesus Christ, the Bright and Morning Star, shall appear in the clouds and we shall meet again. Somehow, I imagine, we shall greet with that old familiar wave. *One day! One day soon!*

In the darkness of death, how bright and glorious is the promise of the resurrection.

> While we walk the pilgrim pathway,
>   Clouds will overspread the sky;
> But when trav'ling days are over
>   Not a shadow, not a sigh.
> When we all get to heaven,
>   What a day of rejoicing that will be!
> When we all see Jesus,
>   We'll sing and shout the victory.
>   —*Eliza E. Hewitt*

D. L. Moody was visiting an industrial exposition in Chicago.[2] On the grounds was a fountain that became a rendezvous for folk. One would say to another, "Will I meet you at the fountain?" The reply would come, "Yes, I will meet you at the fountain!" P. P. Bliss, the gospel hymnwriter, was lured to the place and was inspired to pen these words:

> Will I meet you at the fountain,
>   When I reach the Glory land?
> When you meet me at the fountain,

Shall I clasp your friendly hand?
Other friends will give you welcome;
    Other loving voices cheer,
There'll be music at the fountain,
    Will I meet you there?
Will you meet me at the fountain,
    When I reach the Glory land?
When you meet me at the fountain,
    Shall I clasp your friendly hand?
Other friends will give you welcome;
    Other loving voices cheer,
There'll be music at the fountain,
    Will you meet me there?

*He revealeth the deep and
secret things: he knoweth
what is in the darkness,
and the light dwelleth
with him (Daniel 2:22).*

When darkness veils His lovely face,
    I rest on His unchanging grace;
In ev'ry high and stormy gale
    My anchor holds within the veil.
On Christ, the solid Rock, I stand—
    All other ground is sinking sand.
                        —*Edward Mote*

CHAPTER 2

In the Shadows of Sorrow Glow the Comforts of Compassion

Returning to the spot where we had found our son's body was another difficult experience; yet I found myself doing so several times. In my mind I reconstructed the scene in which Kerry had ended his life.

The spot was located in a small patch of woods. Visible from that location is the parsonage, which lies about thirty yards away, and our church, which could be seen seventy yards farther. There were the remnants of his little fire where he had burned his diary, other unidentifiable personal letters and paper items. He had always been a meticulous notekeeper and letter writer, even as a young boy; and in the ashes we found the charred spiral wire that had bound his notebook. On the ground was his backpack with a few changes of clothing and half a can of Mountain Dew. A box of ammunition was there, opened with one shell missing. The missing shell was encased in the shotgun; the barrel had been sawed off at the grip. With one blast to the head he had ended his earthly life.

In further reconstructing that scene in my mind, I have imagined how he must have been hurting inside. Upon graduation from high school he left immediately for the army under a program where he was granted a $5,000 bonus. He served two extremely difficult years and had been released with a general discharge. He had been married only two years when his marriage fell apart and his heart was broken. A plan had been arranged at the time of the divorce for his wife and him to meet in Chicago on their third anniversary to see if the relationship could be restored. The reunion did not transpire. He had recently lost his job, his car had broken down, and he was faced with a large student loan with no way to meet the obligation. How he must have needed someone to love him, someone who would stop him from following through with his plan of suicide.

All around us are hurting people with many great needs. If a person breaks a leg, we see and sympathize. If a person suffers from bodily injury, we extend our comfort and help because we can see the hurt. What we often don't see is the hurt inside, hidden from the eyes and minds of men; the grinding, aching, longing hurt that wants someone to care.

How great our God is Who knows each individual and loves him with tender compassion. What a message we have to share with the world; we have a God Who loves us and is able to put the broken pieces of life together and make it worthwhile. Jesus said, "I am come that they might have life, and that they might have it more abundantly" (John 10:10).

We will always have many unanswered questions about this suicide. How long did Kerry sit there? Was it at night or in the daytime? Did he sit watching the lights and comforts of home and want to be there? The date of August 24, 1988, was a Wednesday; did he see us going to prayer meeting? How did I pray that night? Was his name mentioned? Was it after the church service, and we did not hear? Why didn't he walk another thirty yards and let us help?

It must be that people who commit suicide think their deed will erase all hurt. It doesn't because the only hurt that is erased is their personal earthly hurt—they must answer to God in eternity. If only a person who contemplates suicide could realize that his hurt is instead multiplied in the lives of others.

It is multiplied by the number of people who knew him. It is multiplied by the number of people who loved him. The hurt increases with the memory of every little hug or kiss or laugh.

Grief produces groanings that are extremely hard to bear. Who is really sufficient and able to bear such a burden? The hurt is deep and indescribable. Is there any light for such darkness? Does anyone understand or care?

A Heavenly Father Knows and Cares

A wonderful comfort is available to each of us who has Jesus Christ as Savior. We must realize that the first heart to experience hurt was God's heart. The day that Adam and Eve chose the path of sin, God's heart ached not only because of His holiness and purity, but also because He knew that from that act of disobedience the human race would be plunged into all the consequences of sin. Death, pain, illness, toil, prisons, hospitals, cemeteries—tears of every description began to flow with Adam's choice to sin. God was right when He declared in Proverbs 13:15, "The way of transgressors is hard." This fact my son was to learn; this defeat he was to experience.

Because of God's hurting heart for the world, God sent His only begotten Son, Jesus Christ, into the world to bear the just judgment for our sin. When an individual trusts Jesus Christ as his own personal Savior, the judgment for his individual sin is dealt with through Christ's finished work on the cross. When the Savior died, He died unto sin once. His death is sufficient for the whole world. As the first man Adam brought ruin, defeat and death to the world, so Jesus Christ, the second Adam, brought victory, life and righteousness (Romans 5:17–20).

Only those who have passed through the dark hours know the beauty of a loving Heavenly Father. Many times I have tried to imagine how God must have groaned as He turned His face from His Son on the cross. Now I have more understanding. Oh, how my "father-heart" has ached for my son, yet never can I fully comprehend how God's "Father-heart" ached as His Son became the Sacrifice for sin. In the darkness God has allowed me to see a tiny glimmer of His heavenly glory.

> *Blessed be God, even the Father of our Lord*
> *Jesus Christ, the Father of mercies, and the*
> *God of all comfort; who comforteth us in all*
> *our tribulation . . ." (2 Corinthians 1:3, 4).*

The Loving Lord Jesus Knows and Cares

The shortest verse in the Bible is one of the greatest. It is found in John 11:35 and simply states, "Jesus wept." His weeping took place at the tomb of Lazarus, His friend whom He loved. Notice verse 38: "Jesus therefore *again groaning* in himself cometh to the grave" (emphasis mine).

Only those who are brought to the grave of a loved one can understand the meaning of those words, "again groaning." How we have wept ourselves empty, thinking we had no more tears to cry, but a little word or a memory brings the groanings again, and the tears flow once again, pouring out from an overflowing reservoir.

No one understands like Jesus. He was fully human and identified with us in all of our experiences of life. He hungered, thirsted, was weary and participated with all our humanity except our sinning. He lived a perfect life that none of us can live. When an individual accepts Christ's work of redemption by faith, a great transferal occurs. Christ accepts *our* sin, and the repentant believer receives *His* righteousness. What a wonderful transaction! But it did not come without hurt—hurt to the Father and hurt to the Son.

Christ knows all about our deep hurting. Jesus groaned with Mary and Martha, the sisters of Lazarus. He knew of their hurt and groaned with them. Do not think that you are hurting alone. There is One Who hurts with you. Christ's "groaning again" occurs every time one of His children hurts. How do I know? The Bible tells me so in Hebrews 4:14–16:

> *Seeing then that we have a great high priest,*
> *that is passed into the heavens, Jesus the Son*
> *of God, let us hold fast our profession. For we*

*have not an high priest which cannot be
touched with the feeling of our infirmities;
but was in all points tempted like as we are,
yet without sin. Let us therefore come boldly
unto the throne of grace, that we may obtain
mercy and find grace to help in time of need.*

What a wonderful light of comfort in the dark nights of our grief.

Does Jesus care when my heart is pained
Too deeply for mirth and song;
As the burdens press, and the cares distress,
And the way grows weary and long?

Does Jesus care when my way is dark
With a nameless dread and fear?
As the daylight fades into deep night shades,
Does He care enough to be near?

Does Jesus care when I've said good-bye
To the dearest on earth to me,
And my sad heart aches till it nearly breaks—
Is it aught to Him? Does He see?

Oh yes, He cares—I know He cares!
His heart is touched with my grief;
When the days are weary, the long nights dreary,
I know my Savior cares.
                                        —*Frank E. Graeff*

The Loving Holy Spirit Knows and Cares

One of the experiences that comes with grief is weakness. A bodily weakness makes the legs feel limp, but even greater is that inner weakness. As a pastor I had dealt with death many times, but this time death dealt with me.

We must realize that our weakness is not unusual, nor is it necessarily wrong. It is merely a manifestation of the grieving and healing process. In Isaiah 40:30 God instructs us that "even the youths shall faint and be weary, and the young men shall utterly fall." Who, more than youth and young men, possesses strength?

The emphasis of Isaiah 40:28–31 is not our weakness, but rather the strength of God. God is absolute strength (v. 28); He does not faint and will never grow weary of caring for His weak ones. To confess that we are weak is to draw the attention of our all-powerful God. Do you remember how you obtained righteousness from God? It was by admitting your unrighteousness and calling upon Him to supply that which you did not have and could not do. Likewise in our weakness we must realize we have no strength. The apostle Paul accepted his weakness and counted it as an asset.

> *And he said unto me, My grace is sufficient for thee: for my strength is made perfect in weakness. Most gladly therefore will I rather glory in my infirmities, that the power of Christ may rest upon me (2 Corinthians 12:9).*

How could I find strength to go on? How could I bear this load that was placed upon my life? Where could I find help for this weakness? God had the answer. God always has the answer.

> *Hast thou not known? hast thou not heard, that the everlasting God, the LORD, the Creator of the ends of the earth, fainteth not, neither is weary? there is no searching of his understanding. He giveth power to the faint; and to them that have no might he increaseth strength. Even the youths shall faint and be weary, and the young men shall utterly fall: But they that wait upon the LORD shall renew their strength; they shall mount up with wings*

*as eagles; they shall run, and not be weary;
and they shall walk, and not faint (Isaiah
40:28–31).*

Hebrew scholars point out that the word for "renew" in this passage has the idea of "exchange." So we read that those who rely upon the Lord shall exchange their human weakness for His divine strength. Every child of God, every "born-again" one, has two intercessors. He has the Lord Jesus, Who is his intercessor in the courts of Heaven; and he has the Holy Spirit, Who is his intercessor in the courts of his heart. Does Jesus know about our groanings? Indeed He does, and He talks to the Father about us and groans again with us. Likewise, the Holy Spirit knows about our groanings:

> *We know that the whole creation has been
> groaning as in the pains of childbirth right
> up to the present time. Not only so, but we
> ourselves, who have the firstfruits of the Spirit,
> groan inwardly as we wait eagerly for our
> adoption as sons, the redemption of our
> bodies. For in this hope we were saved. But
> hope that is seen is no hope at all. Who hopes
> for what he already has? But if we hope for
> what we do not yet have, we wait for it
> patiently.*
>
> *In the same way, the Spirit helps us in our
> weakness. We do not know how we ought to
> pray, but the Spirit himself intercedes for us
> with groans that words cannot express. And
> he who searches our hearts knows the mind
> of the Spirit, because the Spirit intercedes for
> the saints in accordance with God's will
> (Romans 8:22–27, NIV).*

As a young boy I can remember my mother throwing

a heavy cover across my bed on cold nights. She called it a "comfort." What a help it was from the bitter cold. When Christ left this earth and ascended into Heaven to be our intercessor in the courts of Heaven, the Holy Spirit was sent to be "another Comforter"; not one of a different nature, but one of the very same kind. The Holy Spirit is just like the Lord Jesus. The word "comforter" in the original language means one who is called alongside to help. In our grieving and hurting hearts, the Holy Spirit is that One alongside us we can call on. He indwells every Christian and is the intercessor in the courts of our hearts.

Men design machinery of every description to perform special tasks. This machinery is engineered to do those things that are impossible to accomplish through human strength, whether it be pushing dirt, knocking down walls or lifting heavy loads. Likewise the Holy Spirit, as a Person of the triune God, comes into our lives to push out the hurt, to knock down the walls that keep us from joy and to lift the heavy weights from our grieving hearts.

How blessed and wonderful is the comfort that comes to us in our groanings. He does give treasures in the darkness.

> *Now the God of hope fill you with all joy and peace in believing, that ye may abound in hope, through the power of the Holy Ghost"* (Romans 15:13; see also Romans 8:26–28; 15:19; Ephesians 3:16; 6:17; and 1 Thessalonians 1:5).

Loving Friends Know and Care

Walking is great therapy for those experiencing the darkness of grief; walking provides an emotional release as well as physical exertion. One day soon after Kerry's death, I took my daily walk to town and was stopped by a friend who often crossed my path. He lived in our neighborhood, so we were acquainted. It was unusual for him to call to me from across the street and then walk over to talk with me. It was an effort because the man walks with a cane. He took hold of my arm and extended his sympathies to me. With tears in his eyes and sorrow in his voice he told me of his thirteen-year-old daughter's death twenty-four years ago. He had told me of that event before, but then it was merely an experience he had gone through. This time he spoke differently, or maybe I thought so because I "heard" differently. This time I heard from my heart. His words were, "We know of your loss, and we hurt with you." I had lived in his neighborhood for twelve years, but finally I was one who "dwelt among them." John 1:14 tells us that Christ "dwelt among us, (and we beheld his glory)." I had never really understood this verse until I was experiencing this new, great sorrow.

There is a miraculous comforting element in the Body of Christ, the Church. In our human body, when a finger is smashed, an arm is bruised or an ear is pricked, instinctively the hand comes to soothe and comfort. There is no need for prodding or pleading; it comes automatically. Likewise when one member of the Body of Christ is hurting, the other members come to soothe and comfort. The hand gently rubs the bruise or softens the stinging prick just as the members of Christ's Body lovingly come to soothe one another in gentle care. We shall always remember the love extended to us through our church family at Bethel Baptist Church. From the beginning of our sorrow they embraced us and let us know how they hurt with us.

This comforting ministry requires submission; the hurting one must allow expressions of comforting warmth. Love is expressed in many different ways. Sometimes people do not say or show their love in the same manner as you would, but it is there. People care and they want you to know, so the wounded one must allow the loving members of the Body of Christ to do their work of comforting. Only those who have been through the darkness of grief know how glorious the comfort extended by loving friends is.

Our family shall never forget the warm comfort extended by Pastor Mark and Ruth Mayou, who came that first night to pray with our family. They had lost their son, their only child, in a truck accident. They knew how much the comfort of friends can mean.

Because our son took his own life, I wanted to make certain that none of my other sons were suicidal. A Christian counselor who was located in Kalamazoo, Michigan, about thirty-five miles away, ministered to us in a very loving manner. He gave us not only hours but also days of his time to extend sacrificially the mercies of God. We shall always remember his wise counsel.

Various area ministers came for prayer. Cards and notes of sympathy and encouragement were written to us; each of them was like a special medicine to soothe our wounded hearts. The ministry of sending cards and letters has taken on an entirely new meaning to me.

We especially are thankful for the ministry of Pastor Paul Hubble, who ministered to us so capably at the funeral. He has proved himself to our family as a pastor, counselor and friend.

Fellow believers in Christ let their lights shine on a hurting family that was walking through the valley of the shadow of death. God was glorified! What a glorious light for such a time of darkness.

CHAPTER 3

The Gloom of Guilt—
The Freedom of Forgiveness

O
h, Kerry! My son, my son! Look at what I have done to my son! I did this to my son!" Those words blurted out of my mouth, but more significantly they came from my heart.

The shock of finding our son was a horrible nightmare. For several days we had been complaining about a terrible odor that was surrounding our home. "An animal must have died in the woods near the house," we declared. Our two youngest sons were playing basketball and found the smell unbearable. They decided to go into the woods to see if a deer had died. As they were walking into the woods they saw a man they thought was asleep. The second look let them know he was dead. It was not until a closer look that they realized it was their brother. They came running into the house to tell their mother, "There's a body in the woods...a dead man...it's Kerry!" My wife called my study, and I came immediately. My wife, three of my sons and I walked dreadfully into the woods. There was no mistaking it; this was Kerry! The sight was so horrible it shall never leave my mind. We later concluded that he had been there ten days after his drastic deed. I wanted so much to bend down and pick him up in my arms, but the stench

31

forbade me from going too close. The sight of that putrid body was a sight that haunted us night after night. Our youngest son, seventeen years old and a senior in high school, stated it well for us: "I hate the nights!" When I closed my eyes I envisioned the body.

Equally overwhelming was the memory of my last visit with Kerry. There had been long periods when we did not see him. When he did return though, we loved him and made him feel welcome. As a Christian I could not approve of his lifestyle, but I did not preach to him or try to convert him in his manner of living. He knew two things: I loved him, and I did not agree with his pattern of living.

He had lost his job, and he was having problems with his girlfriend. Also influential to that last visit was how I was feeling. I had been ill and was on medication. I felt irritable. In fact, my family had teased me about my mood.

When Kerry stopped by the house, he was going to look for a job, but the ragged holes in both knees of his jeans told me he would not get hired wearing that attire. I took John to school that morning, and I asked Kerry to ride with me. Though he had not asked, I felt he was wanting to move back home. Before he asked, I informed him, "Kerry, you cannot move back home. You can come to eat, and you can come to shower and clean up; but you cannot move back home." We also discussed a statement he had made—that we did not love him and did not treat him well.

When we arrived back at the house, he was angry and left the property through the woods. I made no attempt to stop him, nor did I tell him that I loved him as I usually had done before.

Memories of that last meeting brought an extremely dark cloud of guilt. Almost always I told him I loved him—but not this time. Why could I not read the desperation in his face? How could I turn away a son who was hurting? Why didn't I get him to a counselor or someone else who could help? Why could I not see that he needed a special love to help his hurting and rejected heart?

In natural death there are feelings of sorrow. In an accident there are feelings of tragedy. A murder brings horror; but suicide brings feelings of utter failure! That is how I felt— a complete failure. I had failed as a dad. I had failed as a pastor. I had even failed as a human being who did not have enough compassion for someone hurting and in need of help. Several accusing fingers of shame pointed at me. Guilt can be an overwhelming cloud. Nothing else is quite so defeating and binding, and if left unchecked it can become destructive.

How to confront the agony of guilt is a question that most survivors of suicide face. Many times they ask, "What if...?" or "If only...," or "Why didn't...?" Usually those questions end with the questioner receiving the blame. We must conclude that none of us is perfect. We all make mistakes. We all sin and fail. It is part of human life.

How do I handle my guilt? Can I be *forgiven?* Yes, praise God! He has made some wonderful provisions for guilt. The first forgiveness, however, must be made for ourselves. I had failed my son in many ways, so I dare not reason that all of the blame rests on him. We may love someone as much as possible and, try as we will, still fail. What we do with our failure and sin is an important part of the healing process.

Many of our feelings of guilt are totally unrelated to the event over which we grieve. Sometimes we carry an assumed guilt that centers around speculation and is based on what might have been if we could reverse time. It is what we wish would have happened. But those are not the things that did happen. We cannot assume guilt for not knowing the future. We are but frail and failing humans. We may blame ourselves for allowing the circumstances through which we lost our loved one, but only God knows the events of the future.

Sometimes we remember past situations with our departed loved one. Our minds are quick to recall our harsh words and wrong attitudes or deeds that were not right. These are the accusing fingers that haunt us, but God always has the answers for the needs of His people.

The Old Testament records an illustration of handling

guilt. David was a "man after God's own heart," yet he failed. God recorded David's sin and its consequences, not because he was a greater sinner than other men, but because every one of us will need forgiveness as David did. Our defeat, shame and guilt require the same remedy as Israel's king required. Psalm 32 records the prayer of David's repentant heart:

> *Blessed is he whose transgression is forgiven, whose sin is covered. Blessed is the man unto whom the LORD imputeth not iniquity, and in whose spirit there is no guile (Psalm 32:1, 2).*

Scholars of the Hebrew language inform us that the basic idea of forgiveness is "to bear, to lift, to lift up, to take away." The removal or the lifting away of the burdens of sin is the basis of relief. However, that lifting and removal cannot be accomplished by the endeavors of the one carrying the burden. That is why we all need a Mediator to bear the load away.

Regardless of how bad or how many our sins may be, the great work of Jesus Christ on the cross gives complete freedom and victory over sin. In the back of my Bible is taped a list of twelve things God has done with our sins. It is there not so much for my counseling of others, but for my own use.

What God Has Done with Our Sins

1. He laid them on Jesus.
   Hebrews 9:28; 1 Peter 2:24
2. He forgave them.
   1 John 1:9
3. He washed them whiter than snow.
   Psalm 51:7
4. He made them as wool.
   Isaiah 1:18
5. He covered them.
   Romans 4:7
6. He atoned for them.
   Romans 5:11

7. He freed us from them.
   Romans 6:7 and 18
8. He removed them from us as far as the
   East is from the West.
   Psalm 103:12
9. He cast them behind His back.
   Isaiah 38:17
10. He cast them into the depths of the sea.
    Micah 7:19
11. He blotted them out.
    Isaiah 44:22
12. He will remember them no more.
    Jeremiah 31:34

—Author Unknown
Source Unknown

Forgiving the Person Who Is Gone

In the process of healing we must experience forgiveness, not only for ourselves but also for our forgiveness of others. My son had lived a life that was totally different from that of our family. He had wounded us by his lifestyle and had hurt us deeply by saying untrue things about us.

Kerry's suicide brought the question, "Why did he do this to us?" We felt temporary anger and resentment for what he had done. It was as though he had put a label on me, "FAILING AS A DAD!" We wondered, How will the church accept his death? A pastor is to be an example to the flock, and his death had marked me, "FAILING AS A PASTOR!" There is a social stigma attached to suicide that is difficult to understand. What effect would this have on the community? My son had marked me, "FAILING IN SOCIETY!" How I resented the fact that my son had ended his own life.

Of course, my feelings of anger were temporary because in reflection I realized that he meant no harm. He had, in fact, come home to end his life because he wanted to be found by people he knew loved him.

Forgiving Others

My son was not the only one who needed forgiveness. People had wronged him. I found myself doing a complete reversal—from accusing him to defending him. There were memories of his military experience. He was never the same after he enlisted in the army. There were occasions he wrote home telling of some of his hardships in military life. A group of men had beaten him up, and we suspected much more. He would not discuss it, but he had been cruelly treated. It was really things outside our family that brought him to the point of wanting to escape life.

Forgiving Yourself

The question changed from, "Can I forgive my son for hurting us?" to "Can I forgive others for hurting him?" to yet the ultimate question, "What about my own guilt?"

> *And grieve not the holy Spirit of God, whereby ye are sealed unto the day of re-demption. Let all bitterness, and wrath, and anger, and clamour, and evil speaking, be put away from you, with all malice: and be ye kind one to another, tenderhearted, forgiving one another, even as God for Christ's sake hath forgiven you (Ephesians 4:30–32).*

My heart had become well acquainted with grieving, but so has God's heart. This passage says that the Holy Spirit is grieved when I sin in thought, word and deed. Sin hurts the heart of God. Consider how my sin has hurt God the Father, God the Son and God the Holy Spirit. The Lord Jesus took upon Himself the awful judgment for my sin. He became my Substitute in paying the penalty of my transgressions. It is in forgiving others that I can show that I, too, have received forgiveness. That is why Jesus said in Matthew 6:14 and 15:

*For if ye forgive men their trespasses, your
heavenly Father will also forgive you: but if
ye forgive not men their trespasses, neither
will your Father forgive your trespasses.*

When I acknowledged the waywardness of my son along with my own failures and accepted the complete provision for forgiveness through Jesus Christ, then I could better understand, acknowledge and forgive the sins of others who had wronged me or my loved ones.

If we have done something to offend an individual, we can follow or obey Scriptural procedure for seeking forgiveness. But how do we handle wrongs committed against a loved one who is deceased? We cannot talk to or contact the dead, but we do have a God Who lives and loves in both worlds.

Visitation hours at the funeral home were scheduled from 7:00 to 9:00 P.M. Our immediate family arrived at 6:30 so we could have some time together before others arrived. How beautiful everything looked that evening. Floral arrangements stood in the front of the room, and various baskets and floral arrangements had also been placed around the room. Kerry's body lay encased in a closed grey metal casket. On top were two large arrangements of flowers. The one from his brothers had a ribbon that read, "TO KERRY—FROM KEVIN & DEB, SCOTT, PAUL, JOHN." The flowers from us simply but meaningfully read, "WE LOVE YOU, SON."

Our family gathered together in front of the casket, and the tears flowed as we silently wept together. My wife and I and our four remaining sons formed a circle, putting our heads together much like a football team in a huddle. It reminded me of the times when we had gathered for our family devotions. We all must have felt the same way, for without a word our circle divided and we stepped close to the casket as though to include Kerry. He would always be included in our family circle. He has affected our lives in so many ways. No longer must I be concerned about seeking my son's forgiveness. He is in Glory with the Lord Jesus. Feelings of guilt, bitterness, unforgiveness, revenge and anger—are all emotions limited to this earthly life. He no longer has any connection with those feelings that bind us. To leave this world is to leave behind all the restrictions and scars of sin as well. Eternity brings with it perfect knowledge (1 Corinthians 13:12; 1 John 3:1, 2).

I led our family in prayer and petitioned God for special strength to minister to those people who were coming to express their love to us. Somehow, God dried up the tears, and I did not weep again until after the funeral. What a wonderful peace God gives to those who are experiencing times of sorrow.

> *Thou wilt keep him in perfect peace, whose mind is stayed on thee: because he trusteth in thee. Trust ye in the LORD for ever: for in the LORD JEHOVAH is everlasting strength (Isaiah 26:3, 4).*

When

When men have pain too hard to bear,
And life is weighed with many a care;
When hope has fled and life seems vain,
And troubles stretch in endless train,
Then—may REST be found.

When men have doubts and seek to find
The answer to the thoughts of mind;
When shadows, grim, becloud the sight,
And souls grope, slowly seeking light,
Then—may LIGHT be found.

When men are tempted to do wrong,
And Satan steals away their song;
When siren voices clamor loud,
And passions, base, hang as a cloud,
Then—may STRENGTH be found.

When storms, tempestuous, wind and hail
The boat of life, so small and frail,
Would ground and wreck where breakers roar,
And all seems lost and hopes no more,
Then—may PEACE be found.

When life's strength ebbs, the race is run,
The western sky sees life's last sun;
When loved ones gather face to face,
And hands are held in strong embrace,
Then—may JOY be found.

> —*Harold O. Gronseth*
> *As published in the*
> Grace Broadcaster *(1969)*

If I say, Surely the darkness shall cover me; even the night shall be light about me. Yea, the darkness hideth not from thee; but the night shineth as the day: the darkness and the light are both alike to thee (Psalm 139:11, 12).

Sun of my soul, Thou Savior dear,
It is not night if Thou be near;
O may no earthborn cloud arise
To hide Thee from Thy servant's eyes!

Abide with me from morn till eve,
For without Thee I cannot live;
Abide with me when night is nigh,
For without Thee I dare not die.

Be near to bless me when I wake,
Ere through the world my way I take;
Abide with me till in Thy love,
I lose myself in heav'n above.

—John Keble

CHAPTER 4

Vision of Victory

Each of us experiences mountains and valleys, moments and places of victories and defeats. Pastor Randy Gilmore had recently moved into our area. God moved him there just in time to minister to our needy family. Randy had been a young man in the youth group of our home church in Crawfordsville, Indiana. It was a special blessing to have Randy pastoring in our area. He was one of the first of many who came to extend the compassions of our loving God. Randy asked with great concern, "Dale, the place of Kerry's death is so near the house. Do you think it will be a problem for you?" I answered, "Yes, it will, Randy." His response was, "Can you mark the spot some way?" My immediate reply was, "No! It is a place of defeat, not of victory."

That place was a momentous place of defeat indeed. That was the spot my son was defeated; that was the spot I was defeated as a father; that was the spot my wife was defeated as a mother; that spot was where my sons were defeated as brothers; that was the spot I was defeated as a pastor. In fact it became known to us as "the spot." When I said to my wife, "I went to 'the spot' today," she knew exactly where I had gone. No explanation was necessary.

There are "spots" in our lives that sometimes haunt us.

It may be a sin we committed or an experience we endured or a situation that overwhelmed us or another individual who brought about our downfall. We think of these painful experiences only as "the spot."

For Peter it was the spot near the comfortable fire in the courtyard; for Moses it was the spot at the rock; for David it was the spot on the housetop; for Samson it was the spot in the lap of Delilah. Abraham knew the spot in Egypt; for John Mark it was at a city named Pamphylia; for Adam it had been the spot at the tree in the Garden of Eden.

How that "spot" had defeated us. It was like a large, dangerous beast encamped in the woods. We tried to raise our windows, but the breeze brought with it a frightening feeling. My younger sons had always enjoyed having their bedrooms near the woods where they could see the birds and hear their morning and evening songs, but now "the spot," being so near, caused them to pull their shades to shut out the view.

It was some time before my wife could return to "the spot." I did not attempt to push her to go, but I let her know that when she was ready I would accompany her if she felt she needed me to go along with her. Finally one day she said she would like to return. We walked slowly down the same path we had followed the day we had identified Kerry. When we arrived at "the spot," we knelt together and carefully analyzed what we thought had happened, what we thought he had been thinking as he contemplated the act.

As I watched my wife, I recalled the wonderful experiences of the day a nurse laid that little newborn son into my wife's arms. Betty had meticulously examined him. She turned him over and over in her arms, looking behind his ears, between his toes and under his arms. There was not one place on him she did not thoroughly inspect. Her examination of his departure was equally meticulous. On the ground we found two bones, probably neck bones or bones from his hands; a tooth, his thumbnail and his scalp—all of which we later buried. What we had intended to be an act of victory was suddenly turned into a deeper defeat.

About two months after Kerry's death I received a phone call from a member of our church. The sound of her voice indicated to me she was hurting. She had every right to hurt. She had buried two husbands, a mother and a father; and now her brother was suffering from terminal cancer. I wanted so much to reach out and turn off the hurt. How great it would have been if I could have said, "Everything will be all right. Your brother will get well, and you won't have to cry again." But I knew that would be false.

Does this sin-cursed and hurting world have any hope? How long must all this go on? Surely somewhere there is a word of hope, a promise that the tears will cease, some prospect of life without the deep ache of sorrow. There is! There is a hope for this world that is so wonderful it is almost beyond human comprehension.

Sometimes our view is narrow and limited. We think only in terms of our immediate surroundings. Only God can give us the hope that is fully comprehensive. We know from our own experiences what it is like to hurt, but we fail to realize that this whole creation is hurting. Romans 8:22 informs us that "the whole creation groaneth and travaileth in pain together." We are only a small part of the hurting. Likewise, we shall participate in even greater victory. This hurting world has some great things ahead.

Consider these promises for the future, which God has pledged for this hurting and dying world.

1. Satan will someday be bound and will not bother us.
2. The curse for man's sin will be removed.
3. Our old sinful natures and habits will be changed.
4. Christ shall be the exalted King of the earth, and He shall rule in righteousness.

But even the millennial earth is but a temporary dwelling place. God's plans far supersede the earthly realms.

Dr. David Otis Fuller wrote these words. Brain cancer had taken the life of his twelve-year-old daughter.

Will it ever cease? Will all this round of misery
and suffering and poverty and sorrow ever come
to an end? Will all that makes nightmare out of a
world of sin for numberless millions ever "fold its
tents . . . and as silently steal away" never to
return to the sons of men to cause tears to flow,
hearts to break, faces to be drawn with pain,
eyes to widen with fear, hair to turn gray or
snow-white, minds to totter and reason to be
dethroned?

Can someone tell us for sure that this will ever
take place? We don't want to be fooled—there's
enough lying and mockery and deception in the
world now. We want truth, we want facts, we
want authority that will speak in such a way we
shall know that this will come![3]

Thank God, a day is coming when these things will be
no more! The book of Revelation lists seven things that one day
will be no more!

1. *No more curse* (Revelation 22:3)! When man sinned,
God told him of the curse upon everything relating to him.
Even nature was cursed. God told Adam and Eve that even the
ground would produce thorns and that by the sweat of his
brow Adam would earn his living. When the Lord Jesus Christ
died on the cross, He wore a crown of thorns on His brow to
identify with our judgment. He came to put an end to the curse.

2. *No more sea* (Revelation 21:1)! God has promised a
day when there will be no more sea. This may refer to the
restless, rebellious masses of humanity who live apart from the
living God. "But the wicked are like the troubled sea, when it
cannot rest, whose waters cast up mire and dirt" (Isaiah 57:20).
Or consider this: Water is that which divides. Seven-eighths of
the earth is covered with water, and it separates the land
masses. John the apostle was in exile on the isle of Patmos. A
barrier of water stood between him and his beloved people. He
declared that one day there will be no more sea to keep him

from the ones he loves. You and I can claim that promise also. We know that presently a sea separates us from our departed loved ones, but one day there will be no more sea, and we will be united with them forever.[4]

3. *No more sorrow* (Revelation 21:4)! Job wrote: "Yet man is born unto trouble, as the sparks fly upward" (Job 5:7). Heartaches of every description have followed man through his history on earth, and being a Christian exempts no one from sorrows. The book of Acts informs us that "we must through much tribulation enter into the kingdom of God" (Acts 14:22). Even Jesus knew tribulation (Hebrews 2:18) and was called "a man of sorrows, and acquainted with grief" (Isaiah 53:3). Jesus instructed His disciples, "These things I have spoken unto you, that in me ye might have peace. In the world ye shall have tribulation: but be of good cheer; I have overcome the world" (John 16:33). Yes, thank God, one day there will be no more sorrow. A barrier will separate us from all grief.

4. *No more pain* (Revelation 21:4)! Think of it! No more pain! Hospitals will have ended their work. The services of all doctors, nurses and medicines shall cease. Think of the multitudes of people who have spent years with a pain-racked body. All of this will be over.

5. *No more tears!* A time of no more tears is coming to this weeping world because "God shall wipe away all tears from their eyes" (Revelation 21:4). We have all tasted the bitter tears of sorrow. Yet we thank God that we have been able to experience them, for they are God's means of soothing our aching hearts. Pity the man who thinks he is too strong to cry, for he can have no release for his misery. Just imagine such a glorious thought that one day there will be no more tears of sorrow!

6. *No more night* (Revelation 21:25)! Those acquainted with grieving and suffering know how long a night can last. But night is also used to refer to spiritual darkness, that opposition to spiritual light. Christ is the light of the world (John 8:12). Only one difference exists between light and darkness—and that is Christ. Long has this sin-darkened world lived without

God's Son. He makes our lives light and fearless. Night brings a shadow of fear as we wait for the dawn. But one day night will be no more!

7. *No more death* (Revelation 21:4)! First Corinthians 15:26 states, "The last enemy that shall be destroyed is death." No one could realistically deny death; it is real and is called the "king of fears." Yes, one day even death shall be destroyed. Christ is the resurrection and the life, and He has conquered death for us (John 11:25; 1 Corinthians 15:57).

The Place of Defeat Claimed as a Place of Victory

Yes, our family hated "the spot." How dreadful it was even to look in that direction, much less to stand there. Kerry's birthday was October 9, about a month and a half after we found his body. How we dreaded that day. People were praying for us as the time approached. My oldest son and his wife surprised us by coming home to visit. What a great uplift their presence brought.

I preached that morning on the victory of the cross. I had also come up with a plan for the day. Since God had planted a tree (the cross) on Golgotha (the place of the skull) where man's sin had brought ruin and death, I also planted a tree. My oldest son and I went to "the spot" and planted a mountain ash. Now when I return to "the spot" I am reminded that out of death comes life, and the place of defeat can become the place of victory. What Christ has done for us on Calvary's cross guarantees the victory for all who place their lives into His hand.

Today we feel defeat, but because of Christ and His work we shall realize the victory! *It is glorious!* Your place of defeat today can become a place of victory by allowing Jesus Christ to be the Lord of your life.

Each time I return to "the spot" I am reminded of God's promises:

*And having made peace through the blood of
his cross, by him to reconcile all things unto
himself; by him, I say, whether they be things
in earth, or things in heaven (Colossians
1:20).*

Look, ye saints! the sight is glorious:
See the Man of Sorrows now;
From the fight returned victorious,
Every knee to Him shall bow:
Crown Him! crown Him!
Crowns become the Victor's brow.

Crown the Savior! angels, crown Him!
Rich the trophies Jesus brings;
In the seat of pow'r enthrone Him,
While the vault of heaven rings:
Crown Him! crown Him!
Crown the Savior King of kings.

Sinners in derision crowned Him,
Mocking thus the Savior's claim;
Saints and angels crowd around Him,
Own His title, praise His name:
Crown Him! crown Him!
Spread abroad the Victor's fame!

Hark, those bursts of acclamation!
Hark, those loud triumphant chords!
Jesus takes the highest station—
O what joy the sight affords!
Crown Him! crown Him!
King of kings and Lord of lords.
                              —*Thomas Kelly*

From Hurting

to Healing

CHAPTER 5

Enriched with God's Goodness

Thus far I have been writing from the perspective of our hurting. Now I shall turn our attention to the process of healing. The first part focused on our sorrow; this second part shall focus on the steps for mending. We have been learning of grief; now we shall learn of growth—growth even through the sorrow and hurt. There is help for our healing, and God intends that we shall come forth as victors for His crown and as gems polished and purified for His glory.

> *But he knoweth the way that I take: when he hath tried me, I shall come forth as gold (Job 23:10).*

The holidays were especially difficult that first year. Kerry's body had been found on Sunday of the Labor Day weekend. Then his birthday came on October 9. Thanksgiving came and went, and we were approaching Christmas with anything but enthusiasm. On December 14 we decided to go to Kalamazoo since we had not really done our Christmas shopping. The weather was terrible, and the roads were treacherous; but it was Saturday, and we did need to finish our

Christmas purchases if we were going to do so.

Highway M-43 between South Haven and Kalamazoo is one of the most dangerous roads in Michigan. We were about fifteen miles from home and were following a car up a gradual but steep hill. A car coming from the other direction fishtailed, slid broadside into our lane and collided with the car in front of us. We watched as they rammed together. The two cars seemed to explode as the glass and parts of the cars flew into the air. In order to avoid being involved in the accident, I ran my car into the ditch and came to a halt about five feet from a road sign and twenty-five feet from the wreck. Immediately I raised my voice in praise, "Thank You, Lord!" Then I noticed more intently the two mangled automobiles crumpled in the road. Steam was coming from their engines, and the broken glass and debris made me aware of how serious the situation was.

Paul, our next to youngest son, was riding in the backseat, and I said to him, "Paul, let's see if we can be of some help in this mess." At that time we were the only ones on the scene, and there were no houses near. As we approached the accident we were greeted with a most horrible sight. I will not go into descriptive details, but the first car encased two teenagers who were killed on impact. In the other car the man and woman were still alive and crying, "What happened? What happened?" Part of the window on the driver's door was broken, and I looked in to see them both injured seriously. The lady's eyebrow had been cut, and her eyelid was drooping. A car from the other direction was also following, and he went to call an ambulance and the police. I ran back to the car where the couple was trapped and tried to encourage them, saying, "Help is coming. Hang on! We have help on the way." Not knowing how seriously they were injured or how long they would live, I spoke to them through the broken glass, "Trust Jesus! Trust Jesus as your Savior!" The gentleman replied, "I am! I am!"

Gradually more people began to arrive, and the needed help did come. Our car was stranded in the ditch, and we could not have left if we had wanted to. In those crisis situations minutes seem like forever. It was approximately three hours before rescuers could cut the crinkled metal from the man and woman and get them to the hospital. The temperatures were bitterly cold, and I could not imagine how they must have been hurting.

The police interviewed my wife, my son and me individually. Our car was towed from the ditch and we headed for home—tired, cold and in shock. The two teenagers were still in their car when we left. The boy, we were to discover, had sat next to our youngest son in school; and the girl's name was Carrie—spelled differently but pronounced the same as our son Kerry's name!

When we were back in our warm, safe home, my son said, "Dad, I didn't need that today!" He was right. It had been only three months since he had discovered the body of his brother, but I reminded him that God had put us there in that scene of tragedy to help people who were in desperate need.

Those experiences make you wonder if you will ever laugh again. You begin to ask yourself, Is there any good in the world? A person can even question the goodness of God, but we need to understand that through all the tragedies and sorrows of life God is still enriching our lives with His goodness.

God is right when He declares, "A little that a righteous man hath is better than the riches of many wicked" (Psalm 37:16). But God loves to make people rich! When He gives things to us, He gives "richly" (1 Timothy 6:17), and they are things to be enjoyed. Thus we are to let the Word of Christ dwell in us "richly" (Colossians 3:16).

God has promised in our text, Isaiah 45:3, that He will give *treasures of darkness* to those going through the night seasons. This verse also promises that God will give *hidden riches of secret places*. How great are the abundant blessings of our God—*treasures and riches!*

It is difficult for us to understand how God can possibly enrich our lives through the experiences of grief, but that is exactly what He wants to do. Perhaps you feel God has robbed you of the thing or person closest to your heart. Does it appear that God does not care that you hurt? Do you reason that you have been cheated out of the most valuable possession of your life?

While we may not now know all the workings and ways of our God, one day we shall understand. The missing pieces will be there, and the unanswered questions of our "whys" shall be given full explanation. Notice the encouragements God gives to us sufferers:

> *Therefore the redeemed of the* LORD *shall*
> *return, and come with singing unto Zion;*
> *and everlasting joy shall be upon their head:*
> *they shall obtain gladness and joy; and*
> *sorrow and mourning shall flee away*
> *(Isaiah 51:11).*

> *For I will turn their mourning into joy, and*
> *will comfort them, and make them rejoice*
> *from their sorrow (Jeremiah 31:13).*

In the experiences of life, darkness often seems to hide the face of God, and then our spiritual riches are hidden; but God has not changed, nor has He altered His character. "The LORD is good to all," declared the psalmist in Psalm 145:9. The real question in our sorrow is whether God is good. Perhaps the real test of our faith amid affliction is to see if we can still conclude that God is good.

> *The* LORD *shall open unto thee his good*
> *treasure (Deuteronomy 28:12).*

> *O give thanks unto the* LORD; *for he is good*
> *(Psalm 118:1).*

> *Thou art good, and doest good (Psalm*
> *119:68).*

Many verses inform us of the goodness of God. Joseph endured much undeserved hardship. His brothers hurt him by selling him to a caravan en route to Egypt. Potiphar's wife tried to seduce him and falsely said that Joseph was the one who had made the advances. Her lies ultimately resulted in Joseph's imprisonment. Even after Joseph prophesied the release of a fellow prisoner, he was forgotten. But God didn't forget Joseph. Eventually he was not only released but was also exalted and became the provider of blessings to those who had wronged him. What conclusion did Joseph come to through all his testings? "God meant it unto good . . ." (Genesis 50:20).

The place of rebuilding and victory for us is in our thinking concerning God. If we can accept the goodness of God, even when our hearts are aching, we are on our way to becoming enriched people.

"For thou, Lord, art good" (Psalm 86:5).

Believe Good Things of God

When in the storm it seems to thee
That He who rules the raging sea
Is sleeping—still, with bended knee,
Believe good things of God.

When thou hast sought in vain to find
The silver thread of love entwined
With life's oft-tangled web—resigned,
Believe good things of God.

And should He smite thee till thy heart
Is crushed beneath the bruising smart,
Still, while the bitter teardrops start,
Believe good things of God.

He loves thee! In that love confide—
Unchanging, faithful, true, and tried;
And let [our] joy or grief betide,
Believe good things of God.

Thou canst not raise thy thoughts too high;
As spreads above the earth the sky,
So do His thoughts thy thoughts outvie:
Believe good things of God.

In spite of what thine eyes behold;
In spite of what thy fears have told;
Yet to His gracious promise hold—
Believe good things of God.

For know that what thou canst believe
Thou shalt in His good time receive;
Thou canst not half His love conceive—
Believe good things of God.

—William Luff
As published in the
Grace Broadcaster
(November 1966)

CHAPTER 6

Hidden Riches
Concealed from the Unsaved

Many years ago a gold prospector believed himself to have found riches at last, but he was starving amid the shifting sand dunes of Death Valley, California. On a piece of paper the old man had scribbled, "DIED RICH!" Later when his body was found, he was hugging a small boulder of metallic-colored rock. It was discovered, however, that the rock was nothing but fool's gold. How sad. He gave his life trying to possess a worthless item.

That prospector is not the only one who has died for worthless "fool's gold." The secret of life is learning to distinguish between true riches and fool's gold.

God says, "Riches and honour are with me; yea, durable riches and righteousness" (Proverbs 8:18). God also has much to say about "fool's gold," and He warns us that the riches of this world have these characteristics:

UNCERTAIN—"Charge them that are rich in this world, that they be not highminded, nor trust in uncertain riches, but in the living God, who giveth us richly all things to enjoy" (1 Timothy 6:17).

DECEITFUL—"And the cares of this world, and the deceitfulness of riches, and the lusts of other things entering in, choke the word, and it becometh unfruitful" (Mark 4:19).

FLEETING—"Wilt thou set thine eyes upon that which is not? for riches certainly make themselves wings; they fly away as an eagle toward heaven" (Proverbs 23:5).

CHOKING—"And that which fell among thorns are they, which, when they have heard, go forth, and are choked with cares and riches and pleasures of this life, and bring no fruit to perfection" (Luke 8:14).

DAMNING—"And when Jesus saw that he was very sorrowful, he said, How hardly shall they that have riches enter into the kingdom of God!" (Luke 18:24).

CORRUPTING—"Go to now, ye rich men, weep and howl for your miseries that shall come upon you. Your riches are corrupted, and your garments are motheaten. Your gold and silver is cankered; and the rust of them shall be a witness against you, and shall eat your flesh as it were fire. Ye have heaped treasure together for the last days" (James 5:1–3).

The twelfth chapter of Luke relates the parable of a rich man whose only interest in life was to increase his riches, and who left God out. Finally the time came for him to die.

> *But God said unto him, Thou fool, this night thy soul shall be required of thee: then whose shall those things be, which thou hast provided? So is he that layeth up treasure for himself, and is not rich toward God (Luke 12:20, 21).*

A great contrast exists between the riches of the world and God's riches. God's riches are

TRUE—"Who will commit to your trust the true riches?" (Luke 16:11).

DURABLE—"Yea, durable riches" (Proverbs 8:18).

PLEASANT—"Filled with all precious and pleasant riches" (Proverbs 24:4).

EXCEEDING—"Might shew the exceeding riches of his grace" (Ephesians 2:7).

GREATER—"The reproach of Christ greater riches than the treasures in Egypt" (Hebrews 11:26).

BLESSED BY GOD—"The blessing of the LORD, it maketh rich, and he addeth no sorrow with it" (Proverbs 10:22).

ETERNAL—"But lay up for yourselves treasures in heaven" (Matthew 6:20).

A flip through your Bible concordance will identify the riches of God with GRACE, GLORY and GOOD. These are the qualities of God's riches, which He desires to give to His children.

> The man who has God for his treasure has all things in one. Many ordinary treasures may be denied him, or if he is allowed to have them, the enjoyment of them will be so tempered that they will never be necessary to his happiness. Or if he must see them go, one after one, he will scarcely feel a sense of loss, for having the Source of all things he has in one all satisfaction, all pleasure, all delight. Whatever he may lose, he has actually lost nothing, for he now has it all in One, and he has it purely, legitimately and forever.[5]

Those without the Lord Jesus cannot understand spiritual truths (1 Corinthians 2:14). Blind men cannot appreciate the beauty of a sunset or the colored hues of a rainbow or the intricate designs of a flower; but men with vision can clearly discern the great hand of God in all the marvels of creation.

Many times God's people are viewed as being "poor people." But a Christian, no matter how meager his earthly goods, is a very wealthy individual. Worldly people tell us we must see things through their eyes, but why should we listen to those who have blind eyes—those who cannot see the hidden riches of God?

The words of Jesus in prayer are not often recorded in the Word of God; but when they are, they are significant. One such prayer is recorded in Luke 10:21:

> *In that hour Jesus rejoiced in spirit, and said,*
> *I thank thee, O Father, Lord of heaven and*
> *earth, that thou hast hid these things from the*
> *wise and prudent, and hast revealed them*
> *unto babes: even so, Father; for so it seemed*
> *good in thy sight.*

Spiritual truths are not discerned by human intellect or social position; they are given by God. Our sorrows are accomplishing eternal riches for us. Though the pleasures may be temporarily hidden, they are true, pleasant, greater, blessed, honorable and eternal.

CHAPTER 7

Hidden Riches
Developed in God's People

One of the professors at the Bible college I attended gave testimony of receiving a ticket from a police officer for speeding. He afterward discovered that his speedometer had been assembled with a wrong gear and was not working accurately. Nevertheless he thanked the officer and later told him that the ticket had been a blessing in disguise because it helped him discover an unknown problem. Oftentimes God's blessings come to us in disguise; what appears to be a penalty is really God's enabling us to see some area where we need help.

Most of us find life centering around ways that make us comfortable, but God's primary concern is to make us holy. He is willing to withdraw a present "comfort" for our eternal enrichment.

Received through Pruning

Chapter 15 of John presents the principles of fruit bearing. We are told that God the Father is the husbandman or farmer; Christ is the stem or root; and Christians are the branches. It is the Father's responsibility to oversee the vineyard; it is Christ's provision to supply sustenance to the branches; and it is each branch's responsibility to bear fruit.

At least four different types of branches are found in the passage.

The branch that bears fruit	(verse 2)
The branch that bears more fruit	(verse 2)
The branch that bears much fruit	(verse 8)
The branch that does not bear fruit	(verse 2)

Notice that the branch that bears fruit should progress until it bears more fruit, and the branch that bears more fruit should progress until it bears much fruit. How does God bring about the increase? Verse 2 tells us that it is through pruning.

Having lived several years in the heart of the great Michigan fruit belt, I have witnessed the process of pruning the trees many times. Knives and saws remove the little "suckers" or twigs and limbs that do not bear fruit and that actually sap the tree's strength and hinder its growth. Spiritual pruning is a process of removing obstacles that hinder fruitfulness. Sometimes it seems the farmer is merciless in the extent to which he executes the pruning, but all the cutting is designed to help the tree become productive.

The Valley

I have been through the valley of weeping,
The valley of sorrow and pain;
But the "God of all comfort" was with me,
At hand to uphold and sustain.

As the earth needs the clouds and the sunshine,
Our souls need both sorrow and joy;
So He places us oft in the furnace,
The dross from the gold to destroy.

When He leads through some valley of trouble,
His powerful hand we can trace;
For the trials and sorrows He sends us
Are part of His lessons of grace.

Oft we shrink from the *purging* and *pruning,*
Forgetting the Husbandman knows
The deeper the cutting and paring,
The richer the cluster that grows.

Well He knows that affliction is needed;
He has a wise purpose in view,
And in the dark valley He whispers,
"Hereafter thou'll know what I do."

As we travel through life's shadowed valley,
Fresh springs of His love ever rise;
And we learn that our sorrows and losses
Are blessings just sent in disguise.

So we'll follow wherever He leadeth,
Though pathways be dreary or bright;
For we've proof that our God can give comfort,
Our God can give songs in the night.
                            —*Author Unknown*
                            As published by the
                            Faith Prayer & Tract League

Beloved of God, you are of ultimate importance to your Heavenly Father. The pruning processes in your life are designed to help you. He is not harming you but loving you in all His ways. David the psalmist said, "It is good for me that I have been afflicted" (Psalm 119:71). We are also told that it is in faithfulness that He afflicts us (Psalm 119:75).

Do not try to understand the "whys" of your great hurt, but determine to yield yourself to the loving hand of God. Some have said the theme of the book of Job is "Why do the righteous suffer?" but I believe the ultimate point of the account of Job's life is *how* we are to respond toward God *when* we suffer.

A. W. Tozer once wrote:

It is doubtful whether God can bless a man
greatly until He has hurt him deeply. Aching
friend, stand fast. Like David when calamity
caved in, strengthen yourself in the Lord your
God (1 Samuel 30:6). God's hand is in your
heartache. Yes, it is!

If you were not important, do you think He would take this long and work this hard on your life? Those whom God uses most effectively have been hammered, filed, and tempered in the furnace of trials and heartache.

Take time to thank your Master for any trials and heartaches in this season of your life. And meditate afresh on James 1:2–12.[6]

Received through Purging

I was once employed by a printing shop to smelt down the lead that was used in the linotype machines. It was vital that the lead be pure in order for it to flow through the linotypes. Therefore, we used a special process to take lead that had already been used for type and to prepare it to be used again. Among the used blocks of lead were pieces of wood, cardboard and paper that had been used as spacers; and among the piles of lead were also all sorts of dirt and debris. We would shovel the lead into the smelting pot along with the wood, paper and other impurities. The lead was melted by the heat of a gas furnace. As it became liquid, it sank to the bottom, and the pollutants rose to the surface. Then we would use a ladle to skim off the unwanted impurities. After a while the lead appeared clean. Not so. A can of chemicals was then placed on a metal rod, and as the smelter stood with his back to the fire, he would drop the can into the pot, causing a virtual explosion. The pot boiled in protest to the added chemicals, and then more corruption floated to the top.

The apostle Peter wrote of a similar purifying process in our lives:

> *That the trial of your faith, being much more precious than of gold that perisheth, though it be tried with fire, might be found unto praise and honour and glory at the appearing of Jesus Christ (1 Peter 1:7).*

*Beloved, think it not strange concerning the
fiery trial which is to try you, as though some
strange thing happened unto you (1 Peter
4:12).*

When we can understand that God is making us eternal
trophies of His grace, then we can understand something of the
purging processes in our lives.

The Refiner's Fire

He sat by a fire of seven-fold heat,
As He watched by the precious ore,
And closer He bent with a searching gaze
As He heated it more and more.

He knew He had ore that could stand the test,
And He wanted the finest gold
To mold as a crown for the King to wear,
Set with gems of a price untold.

So He laid our gold in the burning fire,
Though we fain would have said Him "Nay,"
And He watched the dross that we had not seen,
And it melted and passed away.

And the gold grew brighter and yet more bright,
But our eyes were so dim with tears,
We saw but the fire—not the Master's hand,
And questioned with anxious fears.

Yet our gold shone out with a richer glow,
As it mirrored a Form above,
That bent o'er the fire, though unseen by us,
With a look of ineffable love.

Can we think that it pleases His loving heart
To cause us a moment's pain?
Ah, no! but He sees through the present cross
The bliss of eternal gain.

So He waited there with a watchful eye,
With a love that is strong and sure,
And His gold did not suffer a bit more heat,
Than was needed to make it pure.
                              —*Author Unknown*

Bearing fruit and refining gold are of great concern to
God. Someone has accurately stated that trials either make us
"better" or make us "bitter." Many grow bitter through severe
testings or the loss of a loved one. We must remind ourselves
that trials may be the guarantee of His love. The twelfth chapter
of Hebrews instructs us that every child is disciplined because
the Father loves him. If we have dross without chastening, it
is evident that we are not really born again into God's family.
Determine in your heart not to harbor resentment of any kind.
Ask God to give you a yielded and tender heart that loves Him
supremely.

One of my favorite illustrations is in a book written by
William Culbertson titled *God's Provision for Holy Living:*

> I remember reading a story years ago, called *The
> Sky Pilot,* written by Ralph Connor. Some of you
> may remember it. Mrs. Charles E. Cowman tells
> part of the story in her helpful *Streams in the
> Desert.* She tells about a lass by the name of
> Gwen. Wild and willful, Gwen had had her own
> way all her life. Then through a terrible accident
> she was crippled for life. She became very
> embittered and rebellious. On occasion the Sky
> Pilot (the minister) would visit her. On one of
> these occasions, seeing her in all her ill-will and
> rebelliousness, he said that he wanted to tell her
> a story—a parable, he called it—the parable of
> the canyon. It went something like this:
>
> Once there were no canyons on the face of the
> earth, only open, wild prairies, a great expanse.
> The Master of the prairie, the Lord, walking over

His garden, looked on the great plains and said, "Where are your flowers?" The plains answered back, "Master, I have no seed." So the Lord spoke to the birds of the air, and they carried seeds of every kind and strewed them on the surface of the plains. Soon crocuses and roses and buffalo beans and yellow crowfoot and wild sunflowers and red lilies bloomed all the summer long.

One day, as the Master walked on His great prairie, He said, "Yes, I am well pleased, but where are the clematis and the columbine? Where are the violets and the windflowers, and all the ferns and flowering shrubs?" So once again He spoke to the birds and they carried the seeds and strewed them.

Then once more the Master had to ask, "Where are My loveliest flowers?" The prairie, so the storyteller related, cried sorrowfully, "O Master, I cannot keep the flowers. The wind sweeps so fiercely, and the sun beats upon my breast, the seeds wither and fly away." So the Master spoke to the lightning, and with one swift blow the lightning cleft the prairie to the heart. The prairie rocked, groaned in agony, and for many a day moaned bitterly over the black, jagged, gaping wound in its breast.

But a river flowed and brought its waters and carried black mold. Once more the birds brought the seeds and dropped them in the canyon. After a long time the seeds grew, and vegetation decked out the rough walls with soft mosses, trailing vines, and covered the rocks with clematis and columbine. At the foot of the chasm grew trees, and at the foot of the trees grew violets, windflowers, maidenhair. It was the Master's favourite place.

The Sky Pilot told the story to Gwen. Then he said, "I'd like to read a verse of Scripture, and I'll

change a word or two. 'The flowers of the Spirit
are love, joy, peace, longsuffering, gentleness. . . .'
Gwen, some of these flowers—these graces—
grow only in the canyon."

Somehow the parable spoke to the heart of
Gwen, and she said, "Which are the canyon
flowers, Sky Pilot?" He answered, "Gentleness,
meekness, longsuffering." And Gwen sobbed,
"There are no flowers in my canyon, only rough,
rugged rocks." The Sky Pilot spoke assuringly,
"Gwen, someday they'll grow."

You know, if we take as from the Lord the
tragedy that comes, the sorrow that we know, the
burden that we bear, God will cause these
flowers to grow in us, because whom He loves
He chastens, and scourges every son whom He
receives, that we may become partakers of His
holiness.[7]

In the Crucible

Out from the mine and the darkness,
Out from the damp and the mold,
Out from the fiery furnace,
Cometh each grain of gold.
Crushed into atoms and leveled
Down to the humblest dust,
With never a heart to pity,
With never a hand to trust.

Molten and hammered and beaten,
Seemeth it ne'er to be done.
Oh! 'twere a mercy to leave it
Down in the damp and the mold:
If this is the glory of living,
Then better to be dross than gold.
Under the press and the roller,
Into the jaws of the mint,

Stamped with the emblem of freedom
With never a flaw or a dint;
Oh! what a joy the refining
Out of the damp and the mold!
And stamped with a glorious image,
Oh! beautiful coin of gold!

>   *—Author Unknown*
>   *As published by the*
>   *Golden Rule Post Card*
>   *Company*

CHAPTER 8

Hidden Riches and God's Unsearchable Wisdom

A parable is told of a man who suffered from a physical malady and of the doctor who had prescribed that the patient soak his aching body in hot, briny seawater. Since he lived relatively close to the sea, he attempted to carry enough water from the sea to fill his own tub. After several trips down to the sea, and as he was bringing yet another bucket of water to his home, a nosy neighbor (as neighbors can sometimes be) called out to him from his window and, pointing to the vast ocean, yelled, "You didn't get it all!" Naturally we know it is impossible to empty the ocean. We say that the waters of the sea are immeasurable and their depths unsearchable.

Several times the Bible uses the thought of "unsearchable" to describe the vast expanse of the qualities of our God:

GOD'S PERFECTIONS—"Canst thou by searching find out God? canst thou find out the Almighty unto perfection?" (Job 11:7).

GOD'S WORKS—"I would seek unto God, and unto God would I commit my cause: which doeth great things and unsearchable; marvellous things without number" (Job 5:8, 9).

GOD'S UNDERSTANDING—"Hast thou not known? hast thou not heard, that the everlasting God, the LORD, the Creator of the ends of the earth, fainteth not, neither is weary? there is no searching of his understanding" (Isaiah 40:28).

GOD'S GREATNESS—"Great is the LORD, and greatly to be praised; and his greatness is unsearchable" (Psalm 145:3).

GOD'S JUDGMENTS—"O the depth of the riches both of the wisdom and knowledge of God! how unsearchable are his judgments, and his ways past finding out!" (Romans 11:33).

GOD'S RICHES—"That I should preach among the Gentiles the unsearchable riches of Christ" (Ephesians 3:8).

The day my family found the dead body of our twenty-five-year-old son we experienced an indescribable and unsearchable hurt. No one could ever express it in words, but equal to the inexpressible hurt was the presence of the *unsearchable God*. What I could not do, He did. What I could not bear, He bore. How can I carry on? I thought. Will this ache ever cease? Does anyone realize the depth of my wound? Unseen by human eyes were the unsearchable riches of the living God.

One of the greatest assets of my life was a godly grandmother who knew the Lord Jesus and lived for Him. Her life had a tremendous impact upon many people even though she was limited. I cannot remember my grandmother ever walking, though she had walked at one time and had mothered six living children. I knew her only as an invalid who suffered severely from a crippling arthritis that left her body deformed. Her knees were drawn up so that she could lie only on one side. Her hands and arms were drawn to her body so that she could not feed herself, comb her hair or even chase a fly from her nose. Her hair had been silver white as long as I could recall. She had lost all her teeth, and her features, though pleasant, bore the marks of pain. My childhood friends were afraid of her, though to me she was very beautiful. She had endured a great deal of pain and agony, yet I do not remember ever hearing her complain about her pain or the terrible limitations upon her life. Oftentimes people would wonderingly ask, "How does she do it?" I did not know then, but I do now. It was because of her relationship to the *unsearchable God*.

Often I would walk into my grandmother's bedroom

and hear her singing some of the simple but worshipful hymns of the faith. She knew firsthand that God was sufficient for all her needs. She experienced riches for which many people would have given many dollars to possess. Her kind of riches, however, are reserved only for those who are in Christ; they are hidden in God. The Bible informs us that the child of God has riches in Glory.

Riches in Heaven

The Believer Has   *Promised In*

A Home in Glory . . . . Philippians 3:20
A High Priest Who Is Compassionate . Hebrews 4:14
A Hope for the Future . . . . Colossians 1:5
A Heavenly Inheritance . . . . 1 Peter 1:4
A Higher Affection . . . . Colossians 1:1, 2
A Hidden Life . . . . Colossians 3:3
A Holy Master . . . . Colossians 4:1
A Heart Anchored to God . . . . Hebrews 6:19
A Hymn of Eternal Praise . . . . Revelation 5:9

Someone has given the account of a preacher who was walking along the beach and who came upon a boy digging a large hole in the sand.[8] Curiously he watched the boy labor, and then he asked the boy what purpose he had for excavating such a large hole. The boy told him he was attempting to dig a hole so big that the tide could not fill it. The interested preacher sat down to watch the project develop. Soon the ocean's waves began to move toward the hole. The first wave reached its fingers into the hole and receded. The second wave came and put its arm around the hole and returned, leaving the empty abyss. The third wave came rolling in and completely covered the hole—not only was the hole filled, but the vast ocean of water was still untouched.

No matter how great the needs of our lives are, God's grace is more than sufficient to fill the great vacuums. When we have been tested to the extreme, we find God is still there and He is still sufficient for our needs. How many times have we said, "I can go no further," only to find that God gives grace to take yet another step, to go another day or to bear another burden. When we have gone through some severe testing, we should be reminded concerning God's grace that we didn't begin to exhaust it. He has more—much more! There will never be holes in our lives so deep that God cannot fill them. There is no hurt so great that God cannot help us.

Oh, how unsearchable God is. We cannot measure all of Him, but we measure Him to the extent our needs admit Him. We can know that He is as deep as our sorrow and as wide as our testings. We can measure Him from eternity past to eternity future, and we can never find anything greater than our God.

What a wonderful privilege it is to be a child of God. Consider these "unsearchables" that enrich the life of every believer:

The unsearchable riches of Christ. . . Ephesians 3:8
His indescribable gift . . . . 2 Corinthians 9:15
The surpassing riches of His grace . . Ephesians 2:7
The surpassing greatness of
    His power . . . . Ephesians 1:19
The love of Christ [that] surpasses
    knowledge . . . . Ephesians 3:19
Joy inexpressible and full
    of glory . . . . 1 Peter 1:8
An eternal weight of glory,
    far beyond all comprehension . . . 2 Corinthians 4:17[9]

> Say not, my soul, "From whence
> Can God relieve my care?"
> Remember that Omnipotence
> Hath servants everywhere.
>
> His help is always sure,
> His methods seldom guessed;
> Delay will make our pleasure pure;
> Surprise will give it zest.

His wisdom is sublime,
His heart profoundly kind;
God never is before His time,
And never is behind.

Hast thou assumed a load
Which none will bear with thee?
And art thou bearing it for God,
And shall He fail to see?

—*J. J. Lynch*
From The Disciplines of Life
by V. Raymond Edman.
Used by Permission
of Victor Books/SP
Publications, Inc.

CHAPTER 9

Secret Places

It is in the secret places that we discover the hidden riches God wishes to bestow upon His children.

Sixteen times the Bible uses the term "secret places." I do not pretend to understand fully the term or the various ways in which it is used, but I do know an intimate and personal relationship with God exists that only His beloved ones know. That intimate place of meeting with God is described in Song of Solomon 2:14. Listen to the longing of the Lord for His beloved one:

> *O my dove, that art in the clefts of the rock,*
> *in the secret places of the stairs, let me see thy*
> *countenance, let me hear thy voice; for sweet*
> *is thy voice, and thy countenance is comely.*

The secret place is not easily reached. It is not by downhill paths and broad roadways of comfort that we arrive at the secret place. The only way to discover it is by following the Lord Jesus, Who has been there many times before, and anyone who chooses to know Him must follow Him there.

For His Affection

You who sorrow know of that place that is unseen by the human eye and unheard by the ear of man; it is a place of comfort, hope and peace.

Lovers may have an intimate rendezvous, and they hold that meeting place as very precious. They think only of meeting to please the one who is the object of their affections. God desires that same affection from His people. We are to have a relationship with our Lord, not to be seen of men but a private one, in secret, to please our Lord. Part of that rendezvous should be prayer with the God Who loves us. We are told that when we pray, we are not to pray for men to hear, but we are to go into our closet and pray to our Father in *secret* (Matthew 6:6).

The prayer life of our Lord Jesus is a pattern for us to follow. One example is found in Mark 1:35:

> *And in the morning, rising up a great while before day, he went out, and departed into a solitary place, and there prayed.*

He found the "solitary" place to pray. It might be reasoned that He rose early because of the tremendous amount of responsibility He would face that day, and indeed it was a heavy schedule. His early rising for prayer might also have seemed necessary in order to seek direction, wisdom and the necessary provision for duties. All of these things are true. However, it would seem the most compelling motivation for the early "secret place" was His desire for communion with the Father.

Of all the reasons why you and I should pray, none is more essential than our desire to commune intimately with our Lord.

Somehow the Savior seems a little nearer,
When I kneel down to pray,
And fellowship with Him a little dearer,
When I kneel down to pray.

A secret place of quiet meditation,
When I kneel down to pray,
Increases all the joy of that relation,
When I kneel down to pray.

I tarry there with Christ a little longer,
When I kneel down to pray,
And rise to face the world a little stronger,
When I kneel down to pray.

I know that He will always hear me,
For He is never far away,
And yet He seems a little closer to me,
When I kneel down to pray.
                    —*A. H. and B. D. Ackley*
                    Used by permission of
                    Word, Incorporated

For His Protection

"He that dwelleth in the *secret place* of the most High shall abide under the shadow of the Almighty" (Psalm 91:1, emphasis mine).

It was late one night when we retired to our beds. It had been a week since Kerry's burial. The bed was usually a welcomed place of rest, but since our son's death the nights had become long and frightful. We had just fallen to sleep when the phone rang only one time and awakened me. When I lifted the receiver and no one answered, I returned to my secure spot and nestled under the warm covers.

The night was especially quiet. There were no barking dogs, no cars passing on the nearby road or any other signs of life. Suddenly the stillness was shattered as we heard a loud shotgun blast about a block away. The sudden noise brought back the tears as we remembered the fatal shot that had ended our son's life.

We did not mention the incident to our sons, hoping they had not heard, but they had; and three days later we talked about how ominous and frightening the sound was.

In the darkness of those nights God gave us wonderful

assurance that He was hovering over our home. Psalm 91 gives the child of God a wonderful promise of His divine protection. For several nights we took turns reading Psalm 91 in our family devotions before retiring.

There is a secret place where God's beloved can hide. In Psalm 27:5 David declared,

> *For in the time of trouble he shall hide me in his pavilion: in the secret of his tabernacle shall he hide me; he shall set me up upon a rock.*

David knew that secret hiding place from experience. First Samuel 19:2 records how Saul was determined to slay David, but Jonathan, Saul's son, warned David saying,

> *Saul my father seeketh to kill thee: now therefore, I pray thee, take heed to thyself until the morning, and abide in a secret place, and hide thyself.*

It is recorded again in Psalm 81:7 to remind us that God does hear those who call to Him from the secret place:

> *Thou calledst in trouble, and I delivered thee; I answered thee in the secret place of thunder. . . .*

There are recesses of the heart that only the living God can see, and He does hear and care:

> *Thou shalt hide them in the secret of thy presence from the pride of man: thou shalt keep them secretly in a pavilion from the strife of tongues (Psalm 31:20).*

> *All darkness shall be hid in his secret places (Job 20:26).*

The hymnwriter wrote, "There is a place of quiet rest, near to the heart of God." At least three great blessings are found in the *secret place*. It is a blessed place because it is a place of prayer, a place of protection and—most of all—a place of God's presence.

Reflections

I thank God for the bitter things:
They've been a "friend to grace";
They've driven me from the paths of ease
To storm the secret place.

I thank Him for the friends who failed
To fill my heart's deep need;
They've driven me to the Savior's feet,
Upon His love to feed.

I'm grateful too, through all life's way
No one could satisfy,
And so I've found in God alone
My rich, my full supply!

> —*Florence White Willett*
> *From* The Disciplines of Life
> *by V. Raymond Edman.*
> *Used by Permission*
> *of Victor Books/SP*
> *Publications, Inc.*

*By his light I walked
through darkness
(Job 29:3).*

Find a Rainbow

It really does not matter
If the day is dark or bright.
I can always make it better,
If my attitude is right.

Sometimes clouds obscure the sunshine.
That's when faith comes shining through:
For I know there is a rainbow,
Just beyond my point of view.

So I've learned to keep on trusting,
Even in the darkest day:
And I always find a rainbow,
That can drive the clouds away.

—Author Unknown
Source Unknown

CHAPTER 10

Four Vital Truths for Those Going through Darkness

I would be remiss if I did not include some positive steps that enable me to be an overcomer. Four vital truths will help those who know the experiences of sorrow and grief.

Walk by Faith

"For we walk by faith, not by sight" (2 Corinthians 5:7). The world in its extension of sympathy will not bear with our grief for long. And our great adversary, the Devil, would be overjoyed if we were to remain defeated by our losses. He would have the victory if we were to allow ourselves to continue our remorse. Please remember that with all of God's comfort and concern for us, He still expects us to get up and get on with our lives.

Psalm 23:4 reads, "Yea, though I walk through the valley of the shadow of death, I will fear no evil." Notice that we are to "walk through," not "remain under" or "stay down in." The shadow of death has a way of holding onto those who cross its borders. It is easy to remain indefinitely in the dark valley, and the only way out is to get up and walk.

It is difficult for us to walk in the dark because we want to know where we are going and how we will reach our destination. Often in death's shadows we cannot see ahead, and fear keeps us from wanting to walk into the future. When we have lost our Christian loved one, we think we must remain in the valley because of him; but we must remember that he is not in the valley of the shadow of death—he is in Glory with our blessed Lord. God desires for us to get up and walk on into the future. Life has much more for us.

The Savior Walks beside Me

The way is rough and stony, and the night is dark and
    lone.
A pilgrim on life's journey, I am far away from home.
A gentle voice assures me, "'Twill be better after while."
The Savior walks beside me as I tread each weary mile.

There is One Who can smooth the pathway, Who can
    make the dark clouds bright.
He has promised to be with us even through the darkest
    night.
And though I fail to see Him in the shadows for a while,
I know He walks beside me as I tread each weary mile.

When bruised and torn with anguish and, though faint, I
    struggle on,
The hours are long and lonely, and the friends we loved
    are gone,
He bids me bear the sorrow; it is only for a while.
And so He gives me courage as I tread each weary mile.

There is balm for every heartache in the gentle Savior's
    love.
There is peace and joy—a mansion in the Father's house
    above.
And though the cross be heavy, there is grace to meet
    each trial.
For the Savior walks beside me as I tread each weary
    mile.

—Hattie Walker
Used by permission of
Hattie Walker

Sing to the Lord a New Song

According to the world's way of thinking, singing and sorrowing do not go together. For the Christian, however, singing is much more than a joyful noise; it is an act of worship and adoration. In Acts 16:24 and 25 the apostle Paul and Silas were thrown into prison for preaching the gospel. They had been severely beaten and then placed in stocks in the inner prison. We are told it was the midnight hour—the time of greatest darkness. Here they were in the most wretched prison imaginable, their feet bound, their bodies bleeding and surrounded by darkness. But this was the hour in which they worshiped God. How did they worship? "And at midnight Paul and Silas prayed, and sang praises unto God: and the prisoners heard them." In their darkest hour they prayed and sang. The words of the songs are not recorded, but the motive for their singing is given—they sang unto God.

Your darkest hour is when you need to sing a song of worship unto our great God. Job 35:10 records these words: "But none saith, Where is God my maker, who giveth songs in the night." Notice that it is God Who gives the songs in the night. Emotionally you have no resources from which to draw forth a song. Physically your sorrow may overwhelm you, and your grief may leave you totally weak. Allow God to sing through your weakness.

Psalm 42 is a song of a weary soul much like the hunted deer that has fled for its life. The psalmist wrote of the experiences of tears and sorrows. He spoke of the heavy billows and waves that overwhelmed him, and then he remembered to worship God in the darkness and testified, "Yet the LORD will command his lovingkindness in the daytime, and in the night his song shall be with me" (v. 8).

Psalm 77:6 reads, "I call to remembrance my song in the night." And God made a covenant with His people in Isaiah 30:29, "Ye shall have a song, as in the night."

The psalmist declared in Psalm 147:1, "Praise ye the LORD: for it is good to sing praises unto our God; for it is pleasant; and praise is comely [proper]."

We will accomplish three things when we sing to the Lord. First, God will be glorified in our worship. Second, the saints will be edified. Third, the "prisoners" will hear our song and want to know God.

Almost every time God gives us a glimpse of Heaven in the Bible, He tells us of singing. In Revelation 5 we are given a view of the throne in Heaven as the Book is opened, and we hear the elders respond:

> *And they sung a new song, saying, Thou art worthy to take the book, and to open the seals thereof: for thou wast slain, and hast redeemed us to God by thy blood out of every kindred, and tongue, and people, and nation; and hast made us unto our God kings and priests: and we shall reign on the earth (Revelation 5:9, 10).*

The closer we draw to God, the more heavenly our singing will be. No doubt this is what is wrong with the music of the world; it is so far from God.

When we consider that death has ushered our loved ones into the melodies of Heaven, we can have a song in our hearts to the Lord. Heaven is a wonderful place, and our saved loved ones are singing there in His presence. Even though we are separated by death, we can join them in "singing unto the Lord."

Against a Thorn

Once I heard a song of sweetness
As it cleft the morning air,
Sounding in its blest completeness,
Like a tender pleading prayer;
And I sought to find the singer,
Whence the wondrous song was born,
And I found a bird, sore wounded,
Pinioned by an ugly thorn.

I have seen a soul of sadness
While its wings with pain were furled
Giving hope and cheer and gladness
That should bless a weeping world;
And I knew that life of sweetness
Was of pain and sorrow borne,
And a stricken soul was singing
With its heart against a thorn.

Ye are told of One Who loves you
Of a Savior crucified,
Ye are told of nails that pinioned,
And a spear that pierced His side:
Ye are told of cruel scourging
Of a Savior bearing scorn,
And He died for your salvation,
With His brow against a thorn.

Ye are not above the Master!
Will you breathe a sweet refrain?
And His grace will be sufficient,
When your heart is pierced with pain;
Will you live to bless His loved ones,
Tho' your life be bruised and torn,
Like a bird that sang so sweetly
With its heart against a thorn?

> —*Author Unknown*
> *Source Unknown*[10]

Shine in the Darkness

A man was walking down the street when he noticed a boy with a mirror. It was evident that the youth was enjoying himself immensely as he held the mirror so that the sun would reflect into a second-story window. The man assumed the boy was irritating someone by the reflection, so he chided him for his apparent mischief-making. The little boy then explained that his little brother was an invalid and could never come outside to play; the only sunshine he could ever see was the little bit the brother could bring him. So using the mirror was only an attempt to bring sunshine into the life of someone who lived in darkness.

You and I should be like this young boy; we should bring light to those in this world of darkness. Hurting hearts surround us. Those without the Lord Jesus do not know of the Light that lifts our hearts.

Philippians 2:15 instructs us that our lives must bring light to others:

> *That ye may be blameless and harmless, the*
> *sons of God, without rebuke, in the midst of a*
> *crooked and perverse nation, among whom*
> *ye shine as lights in the world.*

As the moon has no light source of its own and can only reflect the light of the sun, so believers have no light of their own power but can only reflect the light of the "Son"—Jesus Christ. We are commanded to shine for Him.

> *Ye are the light of the world. A city that is set*
> *on an hill cannot be hid. Neither do men*
> *light a candle, and put it under a bushel, but*
> *on a candlestick; and it giveth light unto all*
> *that are in the house. Let your light so shine*
> *before men, that they may see your good*
> *works, and glorify your Father which is in*
> *heaven (Matthew 5:14–16).*

Malachi predicted the coming Savior and wrote of Him:

> *But unto you that fear my name shall the*
> *Sun of righteousness arise with healing in his*
> *wings; and ye shall go forth, and grow up as*
> *calves of the stall (Malachi 4:2).*

In this hopeless and helpless world God has placed you and me to bring a little "Sonshine." No one is better qualified to minister to others in darkness than one who has himself, "walked through the valley of the shadow of death" and who has found a "new song" to cheer the hearts of all who hear.

All God wants us to do is to take our experiences and share them with others. It is His way of bringing help and hope to them, but it is also God's way of helping us to heal in our own hurting. It will get our attention from ourselves and bring our focus upon the needs of others, but most of all it will help us learn more of the Lord Jesus. The more I give to others, the more I will appreciate what Christ has done for me.

One of my hobbies is gardening. I enjoy preparing the soil, planting the seed, observing the processes of growth, fighting the weeds and finally harvesting the fruit of my labor.

I found an interesting observation in the sunflower. I had always assumed the sunflower was so named because it was round and yellow like the sun. But I noticed that it has a great affinity for the sun. In the morning it points its face east, anticipating the rising of the sun. Its face follows the sun's course throughout the day, and by evening it will be turned completely west as if trying to catch one last glimpse before the sun disappears over the horizon. In the morning it again faces east, eagerly awaiting the first rays of light. Every day the sunflower follows this same course until it becomes so fruitful that it seems to hang its head in humility for what the sun has done in its life.

Now I recognize that I, too, have a need to follow the Son throughout the day. My prayer is that my greatest desire may be to exalt Christ. As the world cannot function without the sun, we must allow the Son to become the focal point of our very being, for we cannot function without Him. We must allow Christ to become the most important thing in life.

Let us covenant with God to be more like the Lord Jesus—to walk through this valley, sing our new song and carry some "Sonshine" into the lives of others.

His Lamp Am I
Matthew 5:16

His lamp am I, to shine where He shall say.
And lamps are not for sunny rooms,
Nor for the light of day;
But for dark places of the earth,
Or for the murky twilight gray,
Where wandering sheep have gone astray;
Or where the light of faith grows dim
And souls are groping after Him.

And as sometimes a flame we find,
Clear, shining through the night,
So bright we do not see the lamp,
But only see the light;
So may I shine—His light the flame
That men may glorify His name.

—Annie Johnson Flint
Source Unknown[11]

Allow God to Use Your Heartache as a Ministry to Others

John Bisagno wrote, "If life hands you a lemon, make lemonade."[12] Even the most bitter or sour experience in life can become a source of sweet blessing to others. Your heartache will be a key to open the doors of other hurting hearts. God will use you if you are willing to turn your bitter experience into an opportunity to refresh someone else; it will require a Christ-likeness that denies self and reaches out to minister (Mark 10:45).

> *Blessed be God, even the Father of our Lord Jesus Christ, the Father of mercies, and the God of all comfort; who comforteth us in all our tribulation, that we may be able to comfort them which are in any trouble, by the comfort wherewith we ourselves are*

*comforted of God. For as the sufferings of
Christ abound in us, so our consolation also
aboundeth by Christ (2 Corinthians 1:3–5).*

I usually do not pick up hitchhikers, but about a month after my son's burial, I was somehow constrained to do so. I pulled my car to the side of the road and motioned for the young man to get in. We opened with the usual conversational greetings. As a pastor I try to avoid informing strangers that I am a minister because it sometimes erects a barrier that prevents effective witnessing. Almost immediately, though, he asked me about my occupation; and when I informed him that I was a pastor, he was pleased—he had been wanting to talk with someone who could help him. He was twenty-five years old and was out of a job; his car was not running; and his wife was involved with another man, which resulted in his moving back home to live with his parents. What a shock it was to realize that his situation was unbelievably similar to my son's. When we reached his destination, I pulled the car to the side of the road and shared Kerry's experiences with him. I exhorted him with the words, "Young man, give your heart to the Lord and serve Him regardless of your circumstances." Before we parted, I had prayer with him and asked God to protect him and keep him. I again challenged him to give his heart to Christ. Two weeks later he called to let me know that he had responded to an altar call in his church and had recommitted his life to the Lord Jesus.

Meeting this young man certainly was not accidental; God had arranged for our paths to meet because He knew I had a message that he needed. It would also be an experience that would encourage me to share the burdens of others. I'm thankful that I have had other opportunities to minister as well, and these resulted because of my aching heart for my son.

Exactly three weeks after Kerry's funeral I was conducting prayer meeting in our church when one of the ladies asked prayer for her neighbor whose son had committed suicide and who was beside herself with grief. Immediately following the service I called the funeral home (the same one where my son had been) and asked the people there if they thought I could help. They told me they thought it was a good idea. Upon my arrival the family was standing around the casket talking of the memories of their loved one. I stepped close and listened silently as they shared the events of his life. When there was a pause in the conversation, I introduced myself as the pastor of Bethel Baptist Church and told them that exactly three weeks earlier my son lay in a casket in this very place, also a victim of suicide. Immediately I had their attention, and for the next half hour I was able to share the glories of the Lord Jesus with them and tell them of the comfort that only He can give. Because I was able to comfort them with the same comfort that had comforted me, they had a positive response.

After a few more months had elapsed, one of the members of our church called to ask if I would visit and comfort another family whose son had committed suicide. When I arrived, I noticed that the police were still there, so I did not go in, as I did not want to interfere with their difficult work; neither would I have been able to minister unhindered. I drove around and prayed for the hurting family. When I returned to their home, I told them who I was, and we silently embraced and wept together; they knew of me and had heard of my son's death. They hurt doubly because this was their second son to commit suicide. They ministered to me as much as I ministered to them.

At the time of Kerry's death we received a comforting note from a man who lived in a town about ten miles away. He was a dedicated Christian and a lay preacher. His son had committed suicide two years earlier. We became friends. How pleased we were when he and his family began attending our church. Often we would meet, embrace and weep together.

One Sunday after the morning service we stepped into my office, and he told me of his family's plan to become members of our church. However, on Tuesday morning he had a massive brain hemorrhage that took his life a week later. His precious wife has gone through the sorrows of two tragic deaths. Is it any wonder that she is such a precious saint of God with a tender heart for others who are hurting? Every time we visit she has special words of comfort for us.

Turning your heartache into blessings for others is a living principle of the great apostle Paul. The theme of the book of Philippians is rejoicing, but the background of this epistle is *suffering*. It was in Philippi where, after Paul preached the gospel of Christ, he and Silas were imprisoned and beaten. When they sang songs of praise to the Lord, they ministered to hurting hearts and were a sweet balm to the others. Paul said in Philippians 1:12:

> *The things which happened unto me have fallen out rather unto the furtherance of the gospel.*

A phone call came for me while I was visiting a family from our church. It was one of my sons calling to inform me that I was needed at the hospital immediately. A nine-year-old girl from our church family had been involved in an accident. Upon my arrival at the hospital, a nurse escorted me to the family. As we walked down those long institutional hallways, another nurse spoke softly to inform me that little Amy had been killed upon impact when she rode her bicycle into the path of an automobile.

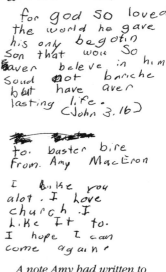

A note Amy had written to the author before her accident

The family had gathered in that small chapel to hear the sad news of the death. My sympathies went immediately to the mother. I watched as she wept openly. The tears flowed from a fountain of a broken heart.

Stepping into that situation was difficult because I knew there were no suitable words. Neither could any reasoning or logic or even prayer replace their loved one.

But I could be there with them in a special way. Thirteen months earlier the salty tears had been mine to taste, and my heartache was much like theirs. Because of the recent death of my son there was a welcome for me in their circle of sorrow. Others could only stand alongside and observe; but the family recognized me as a fellow sufferer, one who was "dwelling among them."

Like the apostle Paul we must allow God to use the things that have happened unto us to further the gospel of Jesus Christ (Philippians 1:12). The tragedy of little Amy was God's opportunity to give the message of eternal life to those facing the reality of death. The funeral service for that little girl was filled with the life of God. Three were saved in the funeral service; and others came to Christ later, including the driver of the automobile, his wife and his daughter. God could penetrate tender hearts with His Word. But those tender hearts came about only through heartaches.

Remember that even though you will never be completely free from the heartache of your sorrow in this life, you can still use your bitter experience to make sweet lemonade to refresh others.

May our great God richly and wonderfully bless your life as you share with others your own treasures of darkness and the hidden riches of secret places.

> *And I will give thee the treasures of darkness,*
> *and the hidden riches of secret places, that*
> *thou mayest know that I, the LORD, which call*
> *thee by thy name, am the God of Israel*
> *(Isaiah 45:3).*

CHAPTER 11

A Word from Mother
by Betty Byers

My husband and I are the parents of five wonderful sons; we awaited every one of them with anticipation and, unless I've forgotten, we didn't feel a shred of disappointment at having all boys. As a mother, I have enjoyed every phase of their lives. The Lord has put a special bond between mothers and sons that nothing can ever take away—not even death. The loss of a child is a tragic event, no matter how it happens or at what age it happens. Perhaps this book can help you walk through a similar sorrow.

If only I could have made time stand still a few weeks before we found Kerry's body. Kerry didn't live at home, so he often stopped by for a short visit. As was his usual custom when he left, he would give me a big hug and a kiss on the cheek, and he would tell me that he loved me. I would always do the same. Little did I know that brief moment was going to have to last the rest of my days here on earth.

I have enjoyed adulthood with each one of my children, except Kerry. Kerry had entered the army as soon as he graduated from high school. After his stint in the army, he lived in another state for a few years. When he did move back home, we had many good times. Kerry worked in a local grocery store as a night stock clerk and would come home early in the morning. Many mornings he and I would go together to a local restaurant for coffee—how I enjoyed those times. Again, little did I know that this precious time would be abruptly cut off. There is no way I can put into words the agony of mind, body and soul our family endured after Kerry's suicide. The hurt was deep because I not only tried to deal with my own grief but also watched helplessly as my other sons sorrowed. And my dear husband was so wounded he could hardly function. Kerry's grandparents also suffered much, as did his aunts and uncles—and the list just goes on. It is hard to understand how a person can feel so unloved when a host of people do love him. However, God doesn't ask us to understand, just to trust Him. He makes no mistakes. As someone told us later, God may have been protecting Kerry and us from some more horrible event in the future in allowing Kerry to take his own life.

Luke 2:19 reads, "But Mary kept all these things, and pondered them in her heart."

Like Mary I have treasures that I have kept and pondered in my heart. Kerry was a very special treasure, and for twenty-five years he added blessings to my life. May I open the treasure chest of my heart and share with you some of my riches. Even though the chest is broken, the treasures are secure.

The Riches of His Personality

God promised to give treasures of darkness, and that is exactly what He gave in Kerry's life. The name Kerry means "dark and mysterious." He lived up to his name. Many times while talking with him I would look into those big brown eyes and wonder what was going on inside. He was always adventurous, just like a little raccoon. In fact, he raised a pet raccoon. He had climbed a huge tree that housed a den of raccoons and came home with two. One he gave away, but the other became his friend. The two almost seemed to understand one another, and with those dancing, dark eyes and cute little faces they even resembled one another.

Mysterious and inquisitive, Kerry would always wander as far as possible and press my mother's limit to the maximum. I recall that as a teenager Kerry would often tell me, "I wouldn't do anything to hurt my mom"—and then turn around and do something he shouldn't do. It seems that Kerry was always the one who would take a mile if you gave him an inch. He would try to stay out just a "little" past curfew. I would lie in bed and pray until I heard him come in. As if being late weren't enough, he would usually stop by our room and tell us one last story before he went to bed; believe me, his stories were usually long ones. Now I can say with some comfort I know where Kerry is and for once, strange as it seems, he is waiting for us to come Home to him. It is a comfort to know that one day we will see Kerry in Heaven with the Lord Jesus. Without that comfort I could not carry on.

I will always treasure his warm, friendly ways. He had many friends, and most people liked him. He was a special gift from God, and sometimes I am afraid I will forget what his face looked like or the sound of his voice or the special way he laughed. But I will never forget the touch of his body or the feel of his kiss on my cheek.

Treasures of Many Happy Memories

As a family we often talk about Kerry as much as we wish. We have many humorous memories to share. I really believe this has helped us in our healing processes. It seems that nearly every day we mention his name in some way. As a mother, I look at my youngest son and see Kerry's smile; our next-to-the-youngest son sometimes wears a shirt that belonged to Kerry; and our next-to-the-oldest son has some of Kerry's same interests—coin collecting, antiques, and so on. Our oldest son lives out of state, so obviously we aren't able to share everyday memories with him. But when we visit, we always share fond memories of Kerry with him as well.

My husband loves to tell the story that has to do with socks. One evening he was baby-sitting when he heard a horrible sound coming from upstairs in Kerry and Paul's bedroom. Kerry was approximately seven years old, and his brother Paul was four. When my husband went up to check on the noise, he opened the door to find the boys having the time of their lives. They had put seven pairs of socks on their feet and were sliding back and forth across the wood floor—an imaginary ice skating rink all their own. The sight was so hilarious my husband wasn't able to scold them. When I say that Kerry was mischievous, that is the kind of activity I am thinking about.

Kerry's brothers love to tell about the time they were caught in a tree. Paul and Kerry were pretending to be mountain climbers. They tied a rope to the back of their belts, but when they were hanging over a limb, they were unable to turn so they could grab the limb and swing up or down. They were stuck there swinging free, one on one side of the limb and the other on the other side. They weren't in any real danger, but their only hope was their three-year-old brother who didn't understand why he should go immediately for their mother. Mother did come and discover their situation and, with a knife, rescued the mountain climbers. Milk and cookies rewarded their hazardous climb.

Among my secret little treasures is a poem Kerry wrote. It wasn't for Mother's Day or any other special occasion; that is what made it special. He just felt like writing a poem and gave it to me. Little did I know that eleven years and five days later he would end his own life.

Mother

Mother, I owe my life to you,
For all my life you have been true.
You wiped the teardrops from my eyes,
And you gave hope to all my sighs.

In my darkest hour and lonesome nites,
You pointed out the way that's right.
You were there in thick and thin,
My heart you couldn't help but win.

You patted my head and wiped my nose,
And even scrubbed between my toes!
You clothed my body on freezing nites,
Kissed my cheek and turned out the lights.

I remember the Mother's Day card I drew,
The year that I was in grade two.
It was awful, no matter how I tried!
I thought you'd laugh; instead, you cried!

You helped me thru lunch and recess days,
You'll no doubt help me when your hair turns gray!
My teenage years did you understand?
Help me now to become a man!

Yet if I work till I'm ninety-two,
I still can't pay back what I owe to you!
But when you're old and your hands get rough,
A hug and a kiss will be just enough!

—Kerry Byers
August 19, 1978

Within that little poem are many hidden little meanings that only a mother and a son can share. The phrase "Helping me through lunch and recess days" was to remind me that Kerry was not much of a fighter, and some bigger boys made life difficult for him during those times. Those are some of the intimate memories treasured by us. Little did I know I would be unable to fulfill the desires of the poem to help him become a man.

When Kerry left for the army, I thought it was the most difficult thing I had been called on to experience, and it was, at that time. He was so young and so inexperienced. I will never know all of the trauma (and there was much trauma) he went through, but I know the army was a different lifestyle from anything he had ever known. I carried a poem in my Bible and often found opportunities to share it with other mothers whose sons were in the military.

To the Boy in the Service
Proverbs 13:1–13

"A wise son heareth his father's instruction: but a scorner heareth not rebuke" (Proverbs 13:1).

Sometimes I used to say to you
When you went out to play:
"Good-bye, my child, be careful, and
Be my good boy today."
And then I tried to school my heart
To trust you to God's care.
Again I send you forth, again
I trust Him; this my prayer:
"Dear Lord, be with this boy of mine
Wherever he may be,
And keep him straight and strong and fine;
Incline his heart toward Thee.

When he is weak, be Thou his strength,
When tired, his resting place;
In battle be his sure defense,
And give to him Thy peace.
Teach him to pray, to seek Thy face;
Ah, Lord, the thought is sweet
That they may meet, his prayers and mine,
Before Thy mercy seat.
Nor for *my* boy alone I pray
In tears before Thy face;
For every mother's son I plead,
Lord, save them by Thy grace!"

—*Martha Snell Nicholson*
Source Unknown[13]

Treasure of God's Special Comfort

When Kerry came home from the army, he was not the same person who had gone. Of course, he did the normal growing up; but I believe things happened to him that wounded him so deeply that he was never able to talk about them. He would always say that someday he wanted to share with us some of his experiences, but he was never able to do it. From that time in his life he began a downhill slide. Some of it was his fault, and some of it was not. But we know all things are in God's control. He could have stopped Kerry from taking his life, but He didn't; and for some reason that I can't understand right now, He allowed the suicide to take place.

It was so difficult to go through Kerry's belongings and decide what to keep and what to throw away or give away. Each brother kept something that held special meaning for him. For me, I would see something that I knew was precious to Kerry and I would think, "Oh, let's put this back; Kerry's children will enjoy this." Then reality would hit, and I would realize there were to be no children from Kerry. We, without a doubt, kept too many mementos; but it was and is very difficult to part with a lot of precious things. So, we have quite a large box stored in our attic full of mementos that represent Kerry's life. Perhaps someday it will be easier to go through things again. Some people are able to dig right in and get rid of their loved one's belongings—that is fine; no one has the answer to whether it is right or wrong—it is a different experience for different people. I am only telling you how it was in my experience and that of our family.

I went back to my work as a billing clerk at our local hospital about two weeks after the funeral. I returned soon in order to occupy my mind. My coworkers were kind; yet I could tell they were also very uncomfortable by my presence. I know it was because they didn't know what to say or if they even should say anything. I understand because I had been in their shoes at other times; and I, too, didn't know what to say. Now when I see someone going through grief, I realize one doesn't have to say anything but give a hug and be there.

Often my husband would ask me to give a reading or recite a poem for special occasions. One Mother's Day after Kerry had left home for the army, I read a little story that was so meaningful to me that I have been unable to read it again publicly. It goes something like this:

Once a little boy was learning to walk, but he kept falling down because his legs were still weak and inexperienced.

Wanting to help him, his mother tied her apron string around his waist and said, "There, my little man, my apron string will keep you from falling and injuring yourself, and you will be able to pull yourself up if you do fall." The little boy did as his mother said. He was tied very close to his mother, and she sang as she worked.

The boy grew slowly until one day he could stand on his toes and see over the window sill. He was fascinated by what he saw. The green grass, yellow flowers and meadows beckoned him to come. The swaying branches of the trees waved for him to follow the singing river and the shining sun. He wanted to climb the purple mountains piled against the sky. He said to his mother, "Mother, untie your apron string, and let me go." But his mother reminded him that only yesterday he had stumbled and would have fallen except her apron string caught his fall.

"You must wait until you are older and stronger," she instructed him. The child did as his mother requested; all went well and his mother sang as she worked.

Slowly but surely the lad grew stronger and taller and left his playthings for older and more mature toys. Often he would stand gazing out the window. One spring morning he noticed the door had been unlatched and stood slightly open. He stood at the threshold looking out at the green grass and the yellow flowers. The waving tree branches motioned to him. He heard the river singing, "COME! COME! COME!" He ran out the door so quickly that the apron string snapped. He kept running, as the broken apron strings dangled behind him. He laughed to himself and thought, "I never knew my mother's apron string was so weak." The mother gathered the end of the broken apron string and hid it in her bosom. But she did not sing again.

The youth ran on to meet the waving branches of the trees and to smell the sweet fragrance of the yellow flowers. He crossed the banks of the singing river and began climbing the purple mountains against the sky. The lad soon discovered that sometimes the path was smooth, but sometimes it was rocky.

At times he had to climb on his hands and knees. Once the path made a sudden turn over the river's bank. Unexpectedly he dashed over the brink of the steep cliff. He would have fallen to the bottom of the precipice; but something caught on the edge of a rock, and he was left dangling over the dangerous bank. When he put his hand behind him to see what had saved his life, he discovered he was hanging from his mother's broken apron string, which was still tied to his waist. "Wow," he said, "I never realized how strong my mother's apron string was!" He pulled himself up and continued climbing on the purple mountain.

Ministering to the Hurting

Wisdom to Understand Affliction
James 1:1–5

> *If any of you lack wisdom, let him ask of God, that giveth to all men liberally, and upbraideth not; and it shall be given him (v. 5).*

The invitation to petition God for understanding is situated in the backdrop of affliction. Temptations and trials often bring questions about our suffering. Why me? Why now? How long? For what reasons do these present afflictions come?

Our text reminds us that we must ask God. Counselors, like Job's friends who have all the answers, abound when we are enduring afflictions. This outline is not an attempt to untie all the knots of suffering. It is merely a feeble attempt to help people look to God during those seasons of hardship and to enable God's people to minister more effectively to the hurting members of the Body of Christ.

I. We can understand the causes of afflictions.
    A. Some afflictions come as normal living processes in a world affected by sin. Note these verses:
        1. Job 5:7: "Yet man is born unto trouble, as the sparks fly upward."
        2. Job 14:1: "Man that is born of a woman is of few days, and full of trouble."
        3. John 16:33: "In the world ye shall have tribulation: but be of good cheer; I have overcome the world."

Sorrow is an actor performing with many masks. Though faces and voices vary, Mr. Sorrow is performing quite well in our churches. We have been called to minister to sorrowing people in their great needs. Consider some of the causes of grief facing our people today: divorce, illness, loneliness, failure, disappointed friendships, family problems, child abuse, addictions, crime, pressures of ministry and death (the king of fears), to name a few.

    B. Some afflictions come as learning experiences, intended to conform us to be more like Christ.

In his book *The Bumps Are What You Climb On* (Baker Book House), Warren Wiersbe relates how the normal processes of life lead us to grow. Growth, simply stated, is changing from one condition to a higher, stronger, better condition. Changes usually occur through rough, rugged falls and disappointments. Victories and successes in life are the stories of how we have overcome failures and problems in life (Acts 20:19; Colossians 1:24; 1 Thessalonians 3:3; 1 Peter 1:6; 2:21; 5:10). Common activities such as walking or riding a bicycle could never be enjoyed without the early processes of falling down and trying again.

    C. Some afflictions come through the chastening purposes of our loving Heavenly Father.
        1. We know from God's Word that chastening is
            a. Universal (Hebrews 12:6-8);
            b. Painful (Hebrews 12:11);
            c. Corrective (Psalm 119:67);
            d. Good (Psalm 119:71);
            e. Fruitful (Hebrews 12:11).

2. Chastening also manifests the character of God as being
   a. Holy (Hebrews 12:11; 1 Peter 1:16);
   b. Faithful (Psalm 119:75);
   c. Loving (Hebrews 12:6).

Perhaps the greatest purpose in all our chastening is to cause us to look to Him and to discover in a fuller measure the greatness of God. In every chastening experience we are exhorted to draw near to God (James 4:8). The farther out on the rod, the harder the stroke. Remember, it is the loving Father Who wants you near Him.

D. Some afflictions are especially chosen by God to demonstrate His glory and grace.

   1. God was wonderfully glorified when our Lord Jesus demonstrated Himself to be the Son of God by healing the blind man (John 9:1–3). The man's blindness was not the result of his sin or the sin of his parents, but was a vehicle to manifest the works of God.

   2. Sometimes God is glorified by delivering an individual out of his suffering by healing.

   3. Most of the time, however, His marvelous grace is given to carry an individual through his affliction (2 Corinthians 9:8).

II. We need wisdom to understand the purposes in afflictions.

   A. Afflictions help to purge us (1 Peter 1:7; 4:12; Job 23:10). God wants our lives to be free from impurities.

   B. Afflictions help to prune us (John 15:1–8). God wants our lives to be fruitful.

   C. Afflictions enrich us (Ephesians 1:7). God wants our lives to be full.

      1. We are enriched through the Word (2 Timothy 3:16, 17). We are fully equipped.

2. We are enriched through the armor (Ephesians 6:10–18). We are fully armed.

3. We are enriched through the fruits (Galatians 5:22, 23; John 12:24–26; 15:11; 1 Timothy 6:17). The fruits are to be fully lived and enjoyed.

D. Afflictions help us to conform to Christ (Romans 8:28, 29). God wants our lives to be fashioned after Christ's (1 Peter 5:10; Hebrews 12:10, 11). We can never be like Christ until we have been wounded by people we love.

Wisdom to Minister to the Afflicted
2 Corinthians 1:3–5

I. The hurting need wisdom to realize the Source of comfort.

A. The Father is a Source of comfort (John 16:27).

B. The Son is a Source of comfort (Hebrews 4:14–16).

C. The Holy Spirit is a Source of comfort (John 14:16).

D. The fellow believer is a Source of comfort (2 Corinthians 1:3–7).

II. The hurting need wisdom to take charge of their emotions.

A. They should take charge over depression (Psalm 42:3).

B. They should take charge over anger (Proverbs 15:1; Ephesians 4:26).

C. They should take charge over guilt (Psalm 51; Psalm 32).

D. They should take charge over fear and worry (Matthew 6:25–34; Philippians 4:6).

III. The hurting need wisdom to help them understand the good intentions of others (Proverbs 25:11; Colossians 4:6).

A. In their hurting, we should help them.

       1. They need to be patient with others (Ephesians 4:30–32).
       2. They need to understand themselves (Psalm 103:13, 14).

    B. In our ministering, we must be cautious.
       1. Don't minimize their sorrows.
       2. Don't restrict the expression of sorrow.
       3. Don't say you understand if you don't.
       4. Don't think you can take away their sorrow.
       5. Don't forget they are not their normal selves.

IV. The hurting need wisdom to take necessary steps for healing.
    A. Walk by faith (book of Job; 2 Corinthians 5:7; Psalm 23:4).
    B. Sing a new song (Psalm 42:8; Acts 16:24, 25).
    C. Be light (Matthew 5:14–16; Philippians 2:15).
    D. Reach out to others (Mark 10:45; 2 Corinthians 1:3–5; Philippians 1:12).

APPENDIX B

Can a Suicide Victim Go to Heaven?

This appendix is not included to be argumentative to those who disagree with the doctrine of the security of the believer. Our purpose is to encourage, comfort and help those families whose lives have been touched by suicide.

Neither does this writing intend to make suicide anything other than it is—a horrible, harmful and hurtful deed. God despises this wretched act, and those who consider taking their own God-given life must realize that they will answer to Him.

Following the suicide death of our son, the question of his eternal destination became prominent in our minds. Is my son in Heaven? That question demanded an answer not only for the satisfaction of my own mind but also for the scores of families whose lives have been and are touched by the suicide of a loved one.

In fact, it is a question that must be answered in the light of many other questions: Can we know for certain that we are saved and on our way to Heaven? Can we know beyond a shadow of doubt that we will make it to Heaven? If we sin, will we be lost? How can we know if we are really "born-again"? How do we handle feelings of doubt and uncertainty? Does the doctrine of the security of the believer lead people to sin? Does a once-saved, always-saved doctrine grant a license to sin and an excuse to neglect righteousness and good works? These and many other questions demand a brief study of the doctrine of the security of the believer.

The Gospel

The word "gospel" means "good news." The message of Jesus Christ brings good news to sinful, dying men. This fallen world constantly faces the consequences of sin: death, disease, divorce and disappointments of every dreaded description. Eternal death and judgment wait at the door of each child of Adam.

The Old Testament records the workings of God in unfolding and fulfilling His wonderful promises of deliverance and blessings to our fallen race. The gospel is called the good news because Jesus Christ fulfilled all those promises. He came to give us life, and life more abundantly (John 10:10). To our darkness Christ is the light of the world (John 8:12), and to our hungering souls Christ is life-giving bread (John 6:32–58). Every individual who has thirsted for just a taste of knowing God can find in Jesus Christ not just a taste, but complete satisfaction for his thirsting soul.

Two Important Truths

1. *Salvation is personal.* Every individual stands alone in his relationship with God. No one else can stand in for him.

Nicodemus was a religious man with an honorable reputation in his community. However, Jesus said to him, "Ye must be born again" (John 3:3, 5, 7). Salvation is granted only to those who have been born again.

My son Kerry can claim no merits to Heaven on the basis of his father's relationship with God. That is one area where he must stand alone before God. But that is also an area in which he has equal privileges. My son's relationship with God cannot be limited by my limitations. My son's salvation is determined by his individual relationship with the Lord.

> *For whosoever shall call upon the name of the*
> *Lord shall be saved (Romans 10:13).*

An experience in my son's life has continually reminded us that he evidently committed his life to Christ. We
believe he made a personal decision of his own volition.

2. *Salvation is eternal.* God repeatedly uses two words
in His invitation to salvation: "eternal" and "everlasting." See
how clearly God explains that those born into His family have
an unending relationship with God:

> *. . . That whosoever believeth in him should*
> *not perish, but have everlasting life (John*
> *3:16).*

> *My sheep hear my voice, and I know them,*
> *and they follow me: and I give unto them*
> *eternal life; and they shall never perish,*
> *neither shall any man pluck them out of my*
> *hand (John 10:27–30).*

Romans 8:33–39 declares with certainty that nothing
can ever separate the child of God from his Heavenly Father:

> *Who shall lay any thing to the charge of*
> *God's elect? It is God that justifieth. Who is he*
> *that condemneth? It is Christ that died, yea*
> *rather, that is risen again, who is even at the*
> *right hand of God, who also maketh interces-*
> *sion for us. Who shall separate us from the*
> *love of Christ? shall tribulation, or distress,*
> *or persecution, or famine, or nakedness,*
> *or peril, or sword? As it is written, For thy*
> *sake we are killed all the day long; we are*

*accounted as sheep for the slaughter. Nay, in
all these things we are more than conquerors
through him that loved us. For I am per-
suaded, that neither death, nor life, nor
angels, nor principalities, nor powers, nor
things present, nor things to come, nor height,
nor depth, nor any other creature, shall be
able to separate us from the love of God,
which is in Christ Jesus our Lord (Romans
8:33–39).*

How much clearer could God make it? When one
becomes a child of God, he is His forever. Nothing in the past,
nothing in the present and nothing in the future can sever that
eternal relationship. One cannot even separate himself.

Believers have the assurance of salvation right now!
Some think one must wait until he dies, then be judged by God
to determine if he will have eternal life. First John 5:11–13
definitely explains that a person who has trusted Christ as his
Savior has eternal life. The verb "has" is present tense. Right now!

*And this is the record, that God hath given to
us eternal life, and this life is in his Son. He
that hath the Son hath life; and he that hath
not the Son of God hath not life. These things
have I written unto you that believe on the
name of the Son of God; that ye may know
that ye have [right now] eternal life.*

God means what He says, and He says what He means.
God says the believer has eternal, everlasting life.

*In hope of eternal life, which God, that
cannot lie, promised before the world began
(Titus 1:2).*

Can a truly saved individual be separated from God
because he has committed suicide? Not according to the clear

meaning of these verses. One principle of Bible interpretation is this: Never use an obscure text to refute a clear text. Philippians 1:6 declares that God does not give up on the believer, and He will continue to work in his life until the Day of Jesus Christ.

In suicide, the individual often has become so distraught with his circumstances and the emotional pressures upon his life that he is mentally not in command of his deed.

Some people say that if a saved person sins, he loses his salvation. Therefore they say that because an individual is unable time wise to confess and receive forgiveness for the sin of self-murder, he must surely be lost. Two things should be emphasized here. First, salvation grants eternal redemption, according to Hebrews 9:12:

> *Neither by the blood of goats and calves, but by his own blood he entered in once into the holy place, having obtained eternal redemption for us.*

Believers are not on probation to see if they will sin again! They have been granted a full and eternal pardon.

Second, what sin separates the believer from Christ? Pride is listed in Proverbs 6:16–19 as the first thing God hates most. Does pride, overeating or a lustful look (as described in Matthew 5:28) cancel God's redemptive work in a life? No. God does hate these sins, but He does not remove salvation because someone who belongs to Him commits them.

Foundation Stones of Salvation

1. *Salvation rests upon the Person and work of Jesus Christ.* Salvation does not result from an individual's own merits or come as a reward for his "good works." Ephesians 2:8 and 9 declare,

> *For by grace are ye saved through faith; and that not of yourselves: it is the gift of God: not of works, lest any man should boast.*

On the cross Jesus became our Substitute in judgment. God the Father laid on Him all of our sins: past, present and future. He not only died for us, He died as though He were us.

> *Who his own self bare our sins in his own*
> *body on the tree, that we, being dead to sins,*
> *should live unto righteousness: by whose*
> *stripes ye were healed (1 Peter 2:24).*

He settled once for all our great sin debt. The Bible explains that Jesus died only one time, and that the one death was sufficient for every sin for every individual who will accept Christ as his Substitute.

> *For by one offering he hath perfected for ever*
> *them that are sanctified (Hebrews 10:14).*

(Notice how the word "once" is used in Hebrews 9:26, 27; 10:2, 10.)

Trusting Christ as our Savior also means we must be willing to accept Him as our Substitute in righteousness. Accepting Him as our Substitute means admitting that our righteousness is insufficient to please God in any way as Romans 8:8 declares, "So then they that are in the flesh cannot please God." Salvation means that we are willing to allow Christ to be our Righteousness.

> *Therefore by the deeds of the law there shall*
> *no flesh be justified in his sight: for by the law*
> *is the knowledge of sin. But now the righ-*
> *teousness of God . . . which is by faith of Jesus*
> *Christ unto all and upon all them that*
> *believe: for there is no difference: For all have*
> *sinned, and come short of the glory of God*
> *(Romans 3:20–23).*

Our entrance into the courts of Heaven is not our own

accomplishment. Our salvation is based upon the Person and work of Jesus Christ in His death, burial and resurrection from the dead (Romans 5:1; 1 Corinthians 1:29, 30; 15:3, 4; Titus 3:5). Christ is now in Heaven.

A boy once disobeyed his father and did not do his chores, which included milking the cows. The father took his son to the woodshed and spanked him. Following the punishment the boy looked at his father and asked, "Now who will milk the cows?" Jesus not only took the punishment for us, but He also "milked the cows." In other words, He was our Substitute in judgment, but He is also our Sufficiency in righteousness.

> *But of him are ye in Christ Jesus, who of God*
> *is made unto us wisdom, and righteousness,*
> *and sanctification, and redemption: that,*
> *according as it is written, He that glorieth, let*
> *him glory in the Lord (1 Corinthians 1:30,*
> *31).*

In no way does our righteousness accomplish our salvation. Neither can our righteousness save us. We are both saved and kept by His grace.

2. *Salvation rests upon the authority of the Bible.* The Bible declares itself to be the Word of God (2 Timothy 3:15–17; 2 Peter 1:19–21). It is more than stories of Bible characters, and it is more than a record book of religious experiences. It is the only God-breathed book. It is the Word of God.

All one knows about salvation is found in the Scriptures. Apart from the Word of God one has no certainty of his relationship with the Lord. This is an important issue because many people have resorted to other sources of authority. Feelings, instead of God's Word, determine the issue for some people. If one has a certain feeling, he must surely be saved. Or if he does not feel saved, then he cannot be saved. But this is not the basis of our salvation and standing in Christ. Rather, the basis is the sure promises of God recorded in His Word.

Other people have made the church their authority. Often people assume their eternal destiny is secure because the church has told them so. They have a false security because they have been baptized or confirmed, have walked down the aisle of a church during an invitation, have shaken a pastor's hand or have been engaged in various religious ceremonies or activities. One's salvation is never determined by what a church declares. One's knowledge of, and experience of, salvation must be based on the authority of the Word of God.

> *Being born again, not of corruptible seed, but of incorruptible, by the word of God, which liveth and abideth for ever (1 Peter 1:23; compare Hebrews 4:12).*

3. *Salvation is guaranteed by the Person and work of the Holy Spirit.* Before the Lord Jesus Christ ascended into Heaven, He promised to send the Holy Spirit, the third Person of the triune God. He also promised that the Holy Spirit would permanently indwell every Christian.

> *And I will pray the Father, and he shall give you another Comforter, that he may abide with you for ever; even the Spirit of truth; whom the world cannot receive, because it seeth him not, neither knoweth him: but ye know him; for he dwelleth with you, and shall be in you (John 14:16, 17).*

The Bible also speaks of the sealing of the Holy Spirit, which signifies His permanent ownership (Ephesians 1:13). The Holy Spirit's indwelling is God's down payment (earnest) of eternal blessings (2 Corinthians 1:22). The Holy Spirit has guaranteed us that He will continue to work with us and to perfect us into the image of Christ until the Day of Christ (Philippians 1:6).

4. *Salvation rests upon the character and veracity of God.* As Titus 1:2 says, "In hope of eternal life, which God, that cannot lie, promised before the world began." If God has made a promise of eternal life, we can rest assured His promise cannot be broken. God did not lie to us about Hell and judgment (Romans 6:23; Hebrews 9:27; Mark 9:43, 44; 2 Thessalonians 1:7–10; Revelation 20:10–15); neither shall He lie to us about Heaven (John 14:1–6; John 11:25, 26).

God is faithful! (Lamentations 3:22, 23; Matthew 5:18; 2 Timothy 2:11–13). His character and reputation are at stake. He is God, and in Him alone are the unfailing, unchanging qualities of perfection. He cannot fail or change—because He is God.

What a wonderful comfort this truth is to the child of God because we can rest secure in Him.

> *Blessed be the God and Father of our Lord Jesus Christ, which according to his abundant mercy hath begotten us again unto a lively hope by the resurrection of Jesus Christ from the dead, to an inheritance incorruptible, and undefiled, and that fadeth not away, reserved in heaven for you, who are kept by the power of God through faith unto salvation ready to be revealed in the last time (1 Peter 1:3–5).*

Distinguishing Terms

The doctrine of the security of the believer does not mean that we have the freedom to sin without restraint or to live unholy lives. Quite the contrary is true. In Romans 6:1 and 2, the apostle Paul answered the question, If we are saved by God's grace, shall we continue in sin? His answer was an emphatic, "God forbid!" Please notice some important differences in the following terms:

1. *Profession vs. Possession:* Many profess to know Christ, but in reality they have made only an outward profession.

> *Not every one that saith unto me, Lord, Lord,*
> *shall enter into the kingdom of heaven. . . .*
> *Many will say to me in that day, Lord, Lord,*
> *have we not prophesied in thy name? and in*
> *thy name have cast out devils? and in thy*
> *name done many wonderful works? And*
> *then will I profess unto them, I never knew*
> *you: depart from me, ye that work iniquity*
> *(Matthew 7:21–23).*

In contrast we find a description of the person who truly *possesses* salvation:

> *And this is the record, that God hath given to*
> *us eternal life, and this life is in his Son. He*
> *that hath the Son hath life; and he that hath*
> *not the Son of God hath not life (1 John 5:11,*
> *12).*

Professing Christ as Savior will accomplish nothing for an individual unless he genuinely is born again of the Spirit of God.

2. *Sonship vs. Fellowship:* Every individual who genuinely receives Christ as Savior has an eternal relationship with God his Heavenly Father. That individual receives two things— his Father's name (1 John 3:1, 2) and life from his Father (John 1:12). That relationship of Father and child will never be broken. A believer is God's child for all eternity, and God the Father will continue to work in His child's life to conform him to the image of His Son Jesus Christ (Romans 8:28, 29; Philippians 1:6).

Fellowship, on the other hand, has to do with the believer's condition within that relationship. When a child disobeys the Father, he loses fellowship, but he does not lose sonship (1 John 1:6—2:2).

The death of my son Kerry made me keenly aware of this truth. Regardless of how Kerry had disobeyed me, he was my son and will always be my son in the flesh. At times the fellowship between us was broken, but there was never a time when he ceased to be the seed of my loins and, may I add, the son of my heart.

3. *Salvation vs. Rewards:* Salvation is clearly a gift of God and is never what we do for God but always what God has done for us in Christ Jesus (Ephesians 2:8, 9; Titus 3:5; Romans 3:20–28; 6:23).

Rewards, on the other hand, are given to the child of God for doing the Father's will. While we are not saved by good works, we are saved to do good works. Ephesians 2:10 states, "For we are his workmanship, created in Christ Jesus unto good works." Salvation is eternal and can never be lost. However, we can lose our rewards (1 Corinthians 3:11–15; 2 Corinthians 5:10; 2 John 8; Revelation 4:11; 22:12). Every Christian's works will be examined at the Judgment, or *Bema,* Seat of Christ (not to be confused with the Great White Throne Judgment, where the lost are sentenced to eternal Hell; Revelation 20:10–15). Things in our lives that have glorified God will be rewarded, and things that have not pleased Him will be burned in the fire of examination. Many people will shed tears and go through great remorse at the Judgment Seat of Christ. Therefore, our goal must be to live godly lives for Christ so that we will hear His welcomed words, "Well done, thou good and faithful servant" (Matthew 25:21–23).

4. *Spiritual Death vs. Physical Death:* It is important to distinguish between these two kinds of death because many people are confused when the Bible speaks of death. Three deaths are spoken of in the Bible.

First, there is "spiritual death." God warned Adam and Eve in the Garden that the consequences of sin is death. He told them that the day they ate of the forbidden fruit, they would die. They disobeyed and partook, but did they die that very day? Not physically, but they did die spiritually. When Adam sinned, he died. When Eve sinned, she died. Therefore all the descendants of Adam and Eve are born dead to God (Romans 5:12). That is why Jesus told Nicodemus in John 3:1–8, "Ye must be born again."

Second, there is "physical death." While Adam and Eve did not die physically the day they first sinned, they did begin a process of death. Before sin, no death process existed in the world. But following Adam's sin the process of death was introduced into this world.

Third, there is eternal death, which awaits those who have been unwilling to receive the Lord Jesus as their Savior. They are those whose names are not written in the Lamb's Book of Life (Revelation 20:10–15).

5. *Condemnation vs. Chastening:* Hebrews 12:3–17 explains God's principles of chastening. He is a loving Father and has pledged that each of His children will begin a process of conforming to the Father's image. Love requires the Father to discipline the children of His love. God always intends chastening to bring wayward children to His loving side.

There is even a point at which the Father will sometimes choose to call a wayward son to eternity by taking his physical life. The Bible calls this "the sin unto death" (1 John 5:16).

No true child of God can continue to live in sin without the chastening hand of the Father. God makes it clear that if an individual can continue in sin without His chastening, the individual is not a genuine child of God (Hebrews 12:6–8).

Nevertheless the believer is in Christ—there is no condemnation to him (Romans 8:1), in contrast to the unbeliever, who "is condemned already, because he hath not believed in the name of the only begotten Son of God" (John 3:18).

Paralleling Truths

God addresses us with language we can understand and uses expressions and illustrations that relate to the world in which we live. The Bible repeatedly describes a believer's relationship with God as being a member of a family and being a part of a body. These important illustrations demonstrate unending unity.

1. *The Family Relationship:* Christ came to reveal to us what God is like. He identified God as Father. He is our

Heavenly Father (Matthew 6:14, 26, 32), Holy Father (John 17:11) and Righteous Father (John 17:25). He is also a loving Heavenly Father with Whom we can have an intimate filial affection (Galatians 4:6).

Birth: When we trust Christ as our Savior, we are, in the Bible's terminology, born. We are "born-again," or born from above. Just as we are born one time in the flesh, we can be born into God's family only one time. If we fail or mess things up in our physical life, we cannot be born all over. Likewise, the "new birth" is a one-time experience.

Growth: Many Christians feel that the initial act of "being saved" is all there is to the Christian life. But if God is our Father, then He desires us to learn many things. God gave us the Bible so we may grow. Just as milk nourishes a baby, a Christian grows by reading the Word of God and living it in his daily life (1 Peter 2:2).

Our Heavenly Father has also pledged to His children that He will care for them, provide for them and walk with them through all their earthly lives. He will never leave us or forsake us according to His promise in Hebrews 13:5. We belong to Him forever. And even though we may be unfaithful to Him, He has promised to remain faithful to us (2 Timothy 2:11–13).

2. *The Body Relationship:* The Bible tells us that when we are saved, we become part of the Body of Christ. Christ is the Head, and believers are individual members (1 Corinthians 12; Romans 12; Colossians 1:18). The truth that God is emphasizing is the inseparable relationship between Christ and His Church. It is an indissoluble union. As the head controls the body, so Christ controls the Church. As the body depends upon the head for direction and life, so the Church depends upon Christ, Her living and ascended Head. If a believer could be lost, then Christ would have missing members of His Body in Heaven. We are assured throughout the Word of God that we are engraven in the palms of His hands (Isaiah 49:16). No members will be missing in Heaven; Christ will have a complete Body (Colossians 1:18—2:9).

END NOTES

1. For further consideration of the bodily resurrection of Jesus Christ, the reader should study *Basic Christianity*, pp. 45–49, by John R. W. Stott, and *Christian Theology*, pp. 120–137, by Emery Bancroft.

2. Paul Lee Tan, *Encyclopedia of 7,700 Illustrations: Signs of the Times* (Garland, TX: Assurance Publishers, 1979), p. 547. Used by permission.

3. David Otis Fuller, *"No More!" "Thank God! No More!": The Seven "No Mores" of Revelation* (Rochester, NY: Interstate Gospel Book Shop, n.d.) p. 9. Used by permission of Institute For Biblical Textual Studies.

4. This truth was shared by Pastor Ted Ertle.

5. Warren W. Wiersbe, *The Best of Tozer* (Grand Rapids: Baker Book House, 1979), p. 19. Used by permission of Baker Book House.

6. A. W. Tozer, *Root of the Righteous* (Camp Hill, PA: Christian Publications, n.d.), p. 137. Used by permission.

7. William Culbertson, *God's Provision for Holy Living* (Chicago: Moody Press, n.d.), pp. 35–37. Used by permission of Moody Bible Institute of Chicago and Moody Press.

8. Tan, p. 504. Used by permission.

9. David C. Needham, *Close to His Majesty* (Portland, OR: Multnomah Press, 1987), p. 152. Used by permission.

10. We were unable to find the source of publication for this poem. We would appreciate any information concerning the source, and we will be pleased to include it in our next edition.

11. We were unable to find the source of publication

for this poem. We would appreciate any information concerning the source, and we will be pleased to include it in our next edition.

12. John Bisagno, *How to Build an Evangelistic Church* (Nashville: Broadman Press, 1972), p. 37. All rights reserved. Used by permission.

13. We were unable to find the source of publication for this poem. We would appreciate any information concerning the source, and we will be pleased to include it in our next edition.